Concusstitution, Welcome to Football

By

Jay Saldi & Timothy Imholt PhD

Concusstitution, Welcome to Football
Copyright © 2019 by Timothy James Imholt and Jay Saldi
Dallas, Texas
For information on this and any book by the authors contact
Tim@TimothyImholt.com

ISBN-13: **978-0-9991073-9-3**
ISBN-10: 0-9991073-9-9

No part of this book may be reproduced, scanned, or distributed in any printed or electronic form without permission.

Fiction Books by Timothy Imholt & David Forsmark

The Forest of Assassins
China Bones Book 1 – China Side
China Bones Book 2 – The Bamboo Caress
China Bones Book 3 – The Red Pagoda
China Bones – The Complete Series

Fiction Books by Timothy Imholt and Michael Garst

The Last World War Volume 1: Trial by Fission
The Last World War Volume 2: Trial by Fusion (in preparation)

Nonfiction Books by Timothy Imholt

Toddler Art

Children's Books by Timothy Imholt

A Collection of Mother Goose Tongue Twisters and Nursery Rhymes

Nonfiction Books by Timothy Imholt & Michael Garst

The Layman's United States Constitution
The Layman's Articles of Confederation
Laughing at a Military Enlistment

Classics with Timothy Imholt Editor/Contributions

A Study in Scarlet with Annotations
The Sign of the Four with Annotations
The Hound of the Baskervilles (Annotated)
The Valley of Fear (Annotated)
The Adventure of Sherlock Holmes (Annotated)
The Memoirs of Sherlock Holmes (Annotated)
A Princess of Mars (Annotated)

Nonfiction Books by Timothy Imholt and Tom Duggan

The Fighting Spirit: Lowell, Bobby Christakos, and The Acre

Nonfiction Books by Timothy Imholt and Jay Saldi

Concusstitution: Welcome to Football

Preface

Who are we?

Why are we going on this crusade?

Most importantly…Can the controversy, much less the safety concerns surrounding concussive injuries that exist in a contact sport that has players the size and speed of those now playing American football, be reduced if not eliminated entirely.

The first two are easy to answer, the third one takes an entire book with some follow-on discussion to fully consider the possibility. Let's start with the easy stuff.

Jay is a former NFL player. He spent time with both the Dallas Cowboys and Chicago Bears during his 9-year professional career, while his college years were spent at the University of South Carolina (Go Gamecocks!). During that time, he played with some of the best coaches to ever set foot on the field and had the honor of playing with one of the best-known, most widely respected Quarterbacks of all time.

When he left college as an NFL hopeful he was undrafted but was signed as a free agent to the Dallas Cowboys. During his years in Dallas he would play under a head coach by the name of Tom Landry and would lineup in an offense led by none other than Quarterback Roger Staubach (yes that one). Despite all of that "undrafted" nonsense, he was chosen as the team captain for the Cowboy's team that was victorious, beating the Denver Broncos by a score of 27 to 10 in Super Bowl XII.

If that wasn't enough, another one of the highlights of his career was catching the final touchdown pass of Roger Staubach's career, something anyone would remember. After being part of one of the hardest to defeat teams in the league of the time and working together for all those years the two remain friends to this day. They have less hair, and far less color in the hair that remains, but that doesn't change the way people who play the game together connect for a lifetime.

Another interesting career tidbit was that renowned head-coach, and Pro Football Hall of Fame member Mike Ditka was once quoted as saying, "Jay runs the best routes around. He's got the unique situation of being something of a combination of tight end and wide receiver."

All of that is great, but this book is about concussions. You may be asking what Jay knows about the pain associated with playing football? What does he know about the potential for a concussion that exists at every position, on every single play of the game? Well other than multiple career injuries, more than a decade between the NCAA and professional level...ok, that's enough. We won't go crazy making the point. Jay understands what it is like to play at all levels of the sport.

He understands the injuries, as well as the life-long challenges that can arise as a result of being a professional athlete. Especially those that arise from the abuse your body takes. He has either dealt with these problems himself or has helped friends and family (he has sons who also played) deal with them.

Ok, so that answers the Jay question.

Who the hell is this Tim guy, and why do we care what *he* has to say when it comes to head injuries in professional sports.

Tim is a physicist by training, and a combination of writer, engineer, and scientist by profession. Part of being a scientist is the ability to convey complex subject matter to someone that isn't a scientist and additionally to use that deep knowledge of those complex concepts to solve problems. Football, and more generally sports, is nothing in the world but a giant physics (more specifically a kinetic energy) problem.

Injuries occur in any athletic event when the physics of the situation gets all out of whack. That's great, but what does that mean in English. Simply put, once in a while an incident (a collision) in a game overcomes the ability of the human body to tolerate the amount of kinetic energy being transferred someplace it doesn't belong.

Wait a minute! You said this would be in English. Seriously, what the hell does all that mean?

Ok, let's dissect that problem statement and break it into smaller pieces so it is easier to understand.

When two objects (or people) are hurtling at one another with some amount of speed and then collide, the energy of motion (called kinetic energy) is going to go somewhere, it doesn't just disappear. We should examine an everyday example. When two cars have a head-on collision, there is going to be some metal that crumbles. One or both of the cars will suffer a lot of damage. That damage is the result of the kinetic energy being deposited into the cars in a way the cars were not designed to tolerate, and the car or cars not tolerating it very well. If that amount of energy was below the threshold for the car to tolerate based on the materials used for construction the accident would result in no damage. That lack of ability to handle the kinetic energy results in laundry list of auto body parts that need to be replaced. Unfortunately for our athletes we can't just give them a new spine, neck, ankle, knee or brain we ran down to the parts store and ordered.

In the case of football that kinetic energy being dissipated sometimes results in a highlight reel for a defensive player putting someone on the ground in a particularly harsh manner. In some cases, the result is an ambulance ride.

Basically, if we examine this closely, the human body is similar to the car body in at least one subtle way. If you ask it to stop moving too quickly, in other words, go from moving to rest in too short a period of time, or for that matter turn too fast or smack into something too hard, that energy of motion is going to go someplace. Energy doesn't just magically vanish.

Kinetic energy will eventually go someplace. If it ends in your wrist, sometimes your wrist may shatter, as Tim's son discovered on a spectacularly bad monkey bar dismount while in the 2nd grade. But, to be fair he was trying to do something he saw on American Ninja Warrior, and after he healed, he did try the same stunt again and got it right, so it is possible to control kinetic energy. That assumes you fully understand the physics of the situation. Elliot got two things out of that situation, a nice cast that made him the hero of his second-grade class, and he also learned to be more careful, so physics can teach us things, and we can learn from injuries.

If we understand the physics of any situation with enough detail, and the methods people use to play the game, we can work towards finding a way to control where the pesky kinetic energy goes. At the very least make sure it doesn't stop someplace that would be too bad for the long-term health of the athlete involved in that crash. To achieve this goal there may be a safety equipment improvement, or perhaps a game play adjustment development required, but if we don't fully understand it we have no way of knowing if the change will be for the better.

With all of that in mind we should take a moment and apply our small physics lesson to the situation we are here to learn more about and take a closer look at the most dangerous play in football: the kickoff return. During this play we see this kinetic energy dissipation problem demonstrated in the most extreme state typically experienced during any game, in possibly any sport that doesn't involve motor vehicles (NASCAR will always beat the NFL for speed).

You have a guy kick the ball, someone else catches it and that receiving player has plenty of room (probably, unless the kicking team's special teams players are rocket like fast) to get moving at full speed. The kicking team also has enough runway to get moving at full speed. The collisions that result of the two (or more) players have the potential to be very damaging to the human bodies involved, despite all the padding and protective equipment required by the organizing bodies at the various levels of organized play.

Forget all the scientific mumbo jumbo for a second, this is where even some small measure of common sense says that this part of the game is the most dangerous. The fastest speed possibly achieved by the players is the problem in this case. That speed causes all that kinetic energy to be build up, and ultimately dissipated, occasionally in dramatic fashion. That energy release is one of the reasons that the leagues have discussed eliminating this play.

Wait? Eliminating the kickoff? Why? It's a tradition!!!

It's all in the math.

Physics teaches us that kinetic energy is calculated as ½ the mass involved in the motion times the square of the velocity. In other words, multiplied by velocity twice.

Let's take two big guys, 200-lbs or more, wearing full gear, which comes with its own mass, hitting each other at full speed. That's a lot of energy.

Don't believe me?

Ok, stand still in a park, or even the practice field at your local high school, let your best friend (or largest person you know just for fun) run at you full speed, then when they get close hurl their body into yours and knock you to the ground. Do you think it is going to feel like a nice warm hug? No, it's going to hurt.

Now, just to make this more realistic to the game, you run as fast as you can directly at them while they are running at you as fast as they can and try hurling your bodies at one another again.

Oh, wait what about the pads?

Yeah, dream on, because those pads will be a whole discussion later in this book, but let's just say the first hit wearing a set of pads isn't the same as the thirtieth hit. That is especially true if those hits are on the same day. Those pads do occasionally need to be replaced and at certain levels of play are rarely refreshed.

The pads may prevent broken bones (mostly), and some other injuries that would take someone out of the game, but they do not stop the players from feeling a hit.

Don't believe us?

Line up against an NFL defensive tackle sometime, see if you want to try being thrown to the ground, pads or not. Personally, bubble wrap me to look like a Sumo wrestler and maybe you could use me as a tackling dummy (Tim talking not Jay). Remember that hit doesn't happen just once that afternoon, these guys do it time and time again. Practice after practice, season after season.

It may sound like we are against people playing the game. We are not. We just want the reader to have some kind of reference point of understanding for what players go through.

At some levels of play the hits are not that hard. At the NFL level, and increasingly at the NCAA level, they are amazingly harsh.

Also, in this book, we will discuss the evolution of the game, and some of the safety procedures (including rules) that have changed over time. Rule changes are sometimes aimed at playability and enjoyability of the game. Sometimes those changes are geared more toward safety improvements.

I know it sounds like we are moaning and groaning about contact sports and demonizing football because those is the examples we used in our little field experiment described earlier, and demonizing football over the concussion problem (which we haven't really gotten to yet) is a popular thing to do these days. We could have just as easily used hockey in this kinetic energy discussion or boxing or mixed martial arts for that matter. All of those sports have the exact same issues just with different methods of dissipating that kinetic energy.

As a side note, Tim made the mistake while researching a different book of stepping into the ring with a retired professional boxer. If you ever have the chance to do that...don't. You have been warned, and that guy was half Tim's size while being nice. It may have been a calculation error when the scientist started talking smack called the boxer short, like a cute little leprechaun (he was Irish), but you live and learn.

There are solutions to some of the injury problems seen in contact sports at all levels, but there is no silver bullet. A combination of things will make contact sports safer, no single answer ever works to completely solve any physics equation, and by the same token no one rule change will solve all the problems in football. We didn't get to where we are in one step, and we won't get to where we want to be with a single change in some other direction.

So why bother? Why not just ban everything, stop playing football, stop all boxing, cease every mixed martial arts event and call it a day?

Banning things is sometimes viewed as the easy way to take care of a problem.

All the controversy, all the problems would be

solved. No muss, no fuss, just boom, it's all better now, no more injuries as a result of a sport.

First, that would be boring, and the United States, as a society, is never boring.

Second, there is no need. We just need to think long and hard about the problem, until we fully understand it and then we can solve whatever issues need to be solved. If we can send a man to the moon and get him back to Earth safely with 1960s technology (assuming Stanley Kubric didn't really film it on a soundstage somewhere…which he didn't), then we know that it is possible to make sport's related injuries greatly reduce in frequency and severity using 21st century technology.

The rest of our reasoning for trying to solve this particular problem spawns from the belief that there is a beauty and grace to athletics done well. Humans are a competitive species at heart, and we need to express that in some way. If you watch football or hockey or boxing or MMA or any other contact sport you can think of, and have seen it done well, there is a certain beauty hidden amongst the violence. There is certainly something that attracts us to watch and be involved in these things.

In other words, contact sports are not going to leave our society.

How can we be so sure?

We will show that football spawns from two different sports which find their origins with the ancient Greeks and Romans. Therefore, they have been around a long time and they are here to stay. Our quest in this manuscript is to show that done properly, understood fully, the risk of injury while playing these sports can be made minimal. We just need to evolve our thinking a little, not demonize a particular sport, or a league, or a group of team owners, or anything else into being the demon masterminding the entire situation. We just need to be truthful about what can be done, and then we need to make sure that we implement the right set of changes to make the sport both as enjoyable and safe as possible.

Chapter 1
Concussions

Concussions…What are they?

Why do we constantly hear about them in connection to football but not in the news headlines in connection with hockey, or soccer (which has a far greater number of them each year than football), or even basketball which has its fair share?

We are going to make an attempt at answering the questions surrounding the concussion problems in a generic enough way so that the understanding can be applied to any sport. We will then try to tie it to football in a way to make the challenges associated with this particular sport more understandable, and perhaps show a path to prevention, or at least limitation to how frequently they occur. Our ultimate goal being getting to a point as fans that we feel comfortable that the sport can continue to have a viable future for the global audience that looks forward to this diversion from our daily lives appearing on our televisions on Saturdays and Sundays during certain parts of the year.

Put simply, a concussion is a brain injury that, depending on the severity, will eventually heal.

When the healing process is complete, the brain will return to some normalized state, or at least return closely to the state it was in prior to the injury. This will permit the person who sustained the injury to return to their normal life in some reasonable period of time. That return to normalcy assumes this injury is a one-time thing. That may not be the case when it comes to athletes.

Repeatedly sustaining these injuries could lead to long-term problems. Some people in the medical profession have said that after an individual suffers from one concussion, even one that is considered minor your brain will be easier to injure the second time.

In the case of some athletes they may be well beyond their second injury.

Think about that for a second.

Don't just let the words get thrown around without due consideration. A concussion is a brain injury, therefore needs to be considered a serious health concern. There are a lot of injuries that can be considered minor, a papercut, stub your toe, etc. However, when it involves someone's brain, should we ever, even casually consider any injury minor?

Given the length of the war on terror, and all of the news coverage of traumatic brain injuries occurring in soldiers as a result of IED attacks which was on television for years, and then there was the wall to wall coverage we all sat through listening to discussions of concussions in football players, it is only natural that we may become desensitized to these words. However, if it were you, and you knew that you were likely to suffer an injury would you choose your brain as the part of your body to be injured? More likely the chosen body part would be the pinky toe or something equally low on the utility scale.

We need to understand that the brain is just a bodily organ, and we know that those can heal, right?

Well yes, the brain can heal, but it also serves as the center of our nervous system. It controls thought, emotion, memory, and motor skills. In short, it makes us…well us. Without a brain the human body may as well be a snack for some meat-eating creature. The brain makes us who we are, and it allows us to solve problems.

Now, think about any injury you ever had and the healing process. Did you damage a knee playing something as a kid? Is that knee back to 100% the way it was before that injury? Was that injury a major or minor thing? Fairly minor you say, but it still gives you aches and pains? Yes, we experience that pain and suffering from some old injuries ourselves.

Would you really want your brain to have that

same experience?

Have we scared you out of playing contact sports ever again?

Never fear, we will talk you back into it later.

Is it even possible to play contact sports and protect yourself?

Absolutely it is, but some changes will be necessary to improve player safety, and we will discuss those in later chapters.

Will it ever be 100% safe? Absolutely not, but neither is driving a car and people do that all the time.

Let's get back to our discussion of what is a concussion.

The brain consists of many things, among them are small structures known as neurons.

Neurons are cells that transmit information throughout the brain. These transmissions are our thoughts, nerve impulses, senses, commands to our arms to pick up a cup of coffee, and even our memories of how to drive to the local coffee shop and get that cup of coffee. If something has move from one place to another in the brain, neurons are responsible for moving it around. If you read this page, or even if you listened to this on audiobook, you used some neurons in the process.

Someplace in your brain a set of neurons remember what the words mean, and others remember how to read them.

These tiny structures transfer information, solve problems, and retrieve memories using electrical as well as chemical signals. This happens across specialized connections called synapses. If these areas become damaged, guess what, information doesn't travel through them properly. To make things a little more concerning, if they are damaged or destroyed the brain has a very limited capacity for regeneration, and while we humans have figured ways to perform knee replacement surgery with a high degree of success, we have yet to figure out how to replace an entire brain, or even do a simple repair job on a single synapse.

In other words, protect your brain, it is the only one you have, and the only one you are likely to ever have.

Also, hang on to that electrical and chemical transmission of information concept, it will become more important in a minute. Don't forget it, and forgive us for saying, keep those neurons alive.

If our brain is hurt, if it gets a boo-boo, it absolutely can't be fixed with a Band-Aid, or if it suffers some kind of permanent injury, the ability to process information from our senses can become limited. That is at a basic level, but these limitations could be manifested through a variety of symptoms. Our ability to reason, to walk, to talk, to go to the bathroom without help, all could be taken from us. Protecting your brain is that important, and these reasons are why we would like to reiterate that no brain injury should ever be considered minor. These are not the types of injuries you can just walk off.

Can protecting your brain *and* playing full-contact football coexist?

That's what we are going to try to figure out together.

Will we fully answer that the question?

That is for the reader to answer for themselves, we are merely here to supply you with facts and make some suggestions on how things might be made safer. These facts will hopefully allow you to make an informed decision for yourself on the risks versus the rewards.

But wait, there's more!

We will not just give you facts; we will dive into interviews with former players, coaches, and trainers. These are the people who have dedicated substantial parts of their lives to the sport. They have experience with the situation and can give an informed view from an additional perspective.

Let's dive right in and try to understand how a concussion occurs and what that word really means. More importantly, what are the medical implications, specific side effects, not to mention the short-term and long-term impacts that could happen to the person who sustained the injury?

Why does our opinion on this topic matter to anyone?

Recall from the Preface to this book that the co-authors have a unique combination of skills and experience.

First, Jay spent almost a decade playing as a Tight End in the NFL. When he was with the Dallas Cowboys he played with Quarterback Roger Staubach and later Danny White under the watchful eye of Coach Tom Landry. This was also during the time that Tex Schramm (one of the most influential guys in the successful transition of football on television) was the General Manager or President. Let's just say that he's been around the sport a very long time and accepted as a well-informed professional by some of the best to ever set foot on or around the field.

Second, Tim, well Tim never played football beyond an occasional game to pass time while in the Army. He is, however, a Physicist (having received a Ph.D.) and spent a lot of years working with, around, and at the Institute for Soldier Nanotechnologies at the Massachusetts Institute of Technology in Cambridge Massachusetts. While there his research partially focused on concussions and Traumatic Brain Injuries (TBI) in soldiers as a result of Improvised Explosive Device (IED) attacks routinely conducted against American troops during the Global War on Terror. During that time, he published peer-reviewed papers and contributed to research on this topic funded by the U.S. Army, the Defense Advanced Research Projects Agency (DARPA) as well as a leading defense contractor.

Putting it mildly, we have both been around concussions and concussed people for a long time. In fact, both of us have suffered from more than one concussion in our lives, and we don't just mean the ones where Tim's mother smacked him in the back of the head for some sarcastic comment.

Outside of Tim's experience, according to Jay, you have not "had your bell rung" until someone like Football Hall of Fame member Randy White (former Dallas Cowboy, sometimes referred to as the Manster, half man, half monster) has tackled you. Apparently, it made no difference to Randy if it was a practice or game, he tackled with a vengeance. More about Randy later. He is someone there should be books written about, but we will try to bring up the relevant parts of his experience in our interview with him later in this book.

Let's get back to the point of this chapter.

The Brain and Skull Relationship

To understand how an injury to the brain happens we must understand certain specific characteristics of where the brain resides inside our body. Obviously, the answer is in the head, but more specifically it is inside the skull.

The skull is a bony structure that gives the head its shape, but it serves a more important function than mere aesthetics. The skull bones are hard plates that surround and protect the brain. In humans the skull is made up of twenty-two different bones. These are very hard structures that nature has put in place to protect our brain, and under normal conditions they do a pretty good job.

In modern football players where helmets to supplement the protection offered by the skull bones.

The helmet worn by football players were originally intended just to stop skull fractures (which weren't commonplace but were known to happen in the sport's early days), and at the time it was not added to a player's equipment to have any effect on concussions. These were originally padded leather, but later evolved into a harder material with interior structures designed to protect the head.

Some of the modern helmets do take concussions into consideration during their design and testing, but this is a more modern shift in this piece of equipment. Therefore, those naysayers who claim nothing has been done to solve this crisis need to consider that some things have been accomplished, steps have been taken, but there is certainly more work needed.

Think about it, when the league started (chapter two will have a brief history of the sport) the helmets weren't there for concussion reasons, merely to stop skull fractures. In fact, for a time there was no helmet worn when playing football. When they were first put in place they were there to stop someone from getting their head split in half. The NFL and organizing bodies at all levels have come a long way with regard to player safety, but most will agree they have further to go, and we'll get to that as well.

The skull in its natural state does a reasonable job of protecting the brain from physical damage. That is in a natural state, by which we mean when only natural threats exist. Natural threats might include falling down, walking into something, being clunked in the head a little bit for some accidental reason, or any other thing that happened to you as a kid on the playground.

Let's examine some cases when unnatural things happen.

When involved in the project at MIT aimed at understanding, and ultimately preventing head injuries for the military Tim did an extensive literature search, and more than one experiment, on the physical properties of the human skull. If to the ultimate goal of a scientific or engineering project is to protect an organ, it makes sense to understand what natural protective measures exist in the human body. Once there is a full understanding of the system already in place, only then we can find the best way to work in conjunction with those protections and build the ultimate protective system that compliments what nature has already put in place. This will result in a layered approach to protection which is a common concept in armor systems, sometimes called compound armor systems, or complex armor systems.

Companies that design and sell bullet proof "stuff" use more than one type of material to provide that protection.

In this case we don't need to stop a bullet, but we need to know what the human body has in place and only then do we know what additional materials are needed.

Let's dig a little deeper into the existing protective system that nature has given human beings.

A general description of bone is two hard plates with a somewhat squishy middle. The hard plates are the white things we see when we look at a skeleton, but inside those hard plates are bone marrow and some other materials that are not nearly as hard as the outside. That is an interesting physical protection system and is easiest thought of as a sandwich structure. Sandwich type structures are also commonplace, not to mention effective when building armor systems.

The hard plates allow for some backward deformation or movement (because of the squishy stuff) in the case of a physical strike, and that gives some time to decelerate an incoming threat (the thing that hit you in the head). When trying to get an incoming threat to stop, no matter if that threat is a bullet or a linebacker, time is necessary and to get that time, one way to get it is with some distance. Any distance gives us time to work with. In other words, bone is a fairly decent armor structure (at least conceptually), even by modern standards, and one that some ballistic materials for stopping bullets, and even certain types of complex IEDs have been designed after that system (obviously using different materials like, but not limited to, steel).

Now that we have some basic knowledge of protective systems, let's dig a little deeper. Remember, to solve a problem we must fully understand that problem, otherwise we may come to the wrong conclusion. Giving someone a system designed to protect them from threats that doesn't defeat that threat can cause more harm than good as it gives the wearer a sense of invincibility. This may lead to the wearer taking risks they wouldn't otherwise take.

Back at MIT, part of that extensive literature search on the nature of the protective system we carry with us every day revealed that bone is somewhat piezoelectric. The term piezoelectric is a fancy way of saying that when you squeeze it, or compress it quickly, it spits out some small electrical impulses. Remember back when we said neurons operate on an electrical and chemical processing principal? With that in mind, what happens to the brain when you electrically shock it? It tends to throw those electrical and chemical processes temporarily out of their normal state.

Is this harmful or beneficial?

There was a day and place (which occasionally still happens, although rarely today) when electricity was introduced into the brain to execute people using the electric chair.

There was also a time when a smaller electrical impulse was used to help "cure" people with some form of mental illness. Medical professionals would strap a patient with some mental problem, bi-polar disorder, schizophrenia, or some other diagnosis, down on a table, then put electrodes on their head and flip the switch.

What is the level where electrical impulses are safe? Certainly, the answer is somewhere above zero, and below the electric chair.

As we write this, we are certain that someone will say that the piezoelectric properties of bone are not nearly strong enough to cause any damage and are certainly not comparable to these other (deadly or therapeutic) levels of an electrical impulse. Taken alone, if that was the only thing going on as the head was being hit hard, we might agree, but that isn't the world we live in. It is a complex system and as a result the so called "silver bullet" cause or solution to a problem rarely exists. As a result, we must consider these electrical impulses as part of the overall behavior of the system.

Yes, we agree that the electrical impulses produced by bone are small. But if you are a lineman playing professional football you get hit a lot. Might those repeated small electrical shocks be a contributing factor to the longer-term health hazards?

Well, maybe.

Is there a solution?

Well, here is the tough part of this topic, the answer is also maybe, but we will talk about that in a later chapter. For now, it is important to remember that these impulses are there and that if it were your brain you might not want to volunteer for fifty or more small electrical shocks to the brain every time you line up to play a game, no matter how big the paycheck. Besides, the overwhelming majority of people playing this game are not at the NFL level, and receive no salary for their efforts.

It doesn't sound like a lot of fun, but we'll give you a hint, it can be solved.

Let's move on from the electrical impulses and look at the situation from a slightly different angle.

The skull is further divided into areas known as the facial bones and the braincase (sometimes called the cranial vault).

The cranial cavity (or vault, which is commonly just referred to as the cranium) is surrounded by a number of structures. The first is the skullcap, which is the rounded top of the skull. Then there are the bones that form the top and sides of the braincase which are the flat bones seen on a skull. These all come together at some joints located on different parts of the head.

There are other, interior structures. These are the ones most people are familiar with which are seen every year in Halloween decorations, and the ones most relevant to this part of our discussion. Given that this discussion is not intended for a medical journal and is meant to serve as a layperson overview, just understand these are general structures and not meant to be all-encompassing in describing the human head. We want to focus on the protective structures, and are not excluding any major structure that is intended to protect the brain.

Why do these things matter to our discussion of football, or other contact sports? How will they help us prevent the number of injuries being reported today?

We started this discussion with a desire to understand the mechanism by which concussions occur. More importantly, from that understanding we want to know how to augment protective gear in order to prevent them, and still be able to enjoy playing or even watching football without worrying about what might happen to someone's brain.

Remember we stated that in order to achieve this

ultimate goal we have to understand the protective systems nature has installed in our heads. Only once we have a reasonable level of understanding can we be concerned with the addons that mankind has invented in the form of safety gear and then we can try to understand if we have done everything possible to prevent concussions. If we haven't done everything technologically possible then we can figure out where we should go from here.

Here is a factoid that is becoming much more widely known than it once was, the brain itself is not actually attached to the skull and doesn't come with any kind of natural shock absorber. It is merely protected inside all those bones, and inside the brain cavity it actually floats in a fluid referred to as the cerebrospinal fluid. As we discussed, it is surrounded and protected by the skull bones that resemble plate armor that one might envision made from steel worn by a knight carried upon horseback as they galloped into battle, but inside that structure is a fluid that in some fashion further protects and cushions the brain.

In that brain-fluid environment, the brain itself can swish back and forth like any other object floating in a liquid.

Think about a physical example of this concept for a moment. Let's say you are driving along in a car (not one filled with water or any other kind of fluid). You come upon an unexpected object in the road, it won't pass beneath your car, there is about to be a collision and you slam on the breaks. Everyone in the car is suddenly pushed forward. In this example, there is no fluid, and I know someone somewhere is saying that if the car was filled with some kind of a fluid it would cushion things and reduce the effect of the impact, and that person would be correct.

However, remember we are talking about what's inside your head. So, when a 225-pound football player is running as fast as they can directly at another 225-pound football player on a kickoff with intent of stopping that players forward motion, at some point a collision will occur. Recall that in the car there were brakes and some deceleration time involved but, in this case, it is an all-out collision of large bodies moving quickly, and these guys aren't hitting the brakes.

In the example with the cars, when two of these fast-moving chunks of metal going down the highway decide to collide, and no one has hit the brakes, some bad things are known to happen. There will be crumpled metal, fenders ripped off, and despite all the safety equipment, there is sometimes going to be an ambulance ride involved. Injuries such as whiplash, broken bones, bleeding, and yes, our old friend concussion may be a result of a vehicular collision.

Now, back to the football/physics discussion (and it really is physics). The collision isn't as severe as some traffic accidents, but more severe than others when the potential damage to the human body is the considered, and much different in how that energy dissipation unfolds. Also recall that this collision isn't something that happens once in a blue moon to each of us driving a car. It happens every single time someone suits up to play the game, and more than once per game. Depending upon the position it could be on every play.

Both are examples of what happens when some amount of kinetic energy is involved in a collision, or as a physicist might say, rapid deceleration. Kinetic energy is referred to as the energy of motion. When you take motion out of a situation that energy must go somewhere, sometimes into the players muscles as he slows down his running, other times into the braking system of the car.

Physicists learned from the work of Isaac Newton that energy can't be created or destroyed. It is going to go someplace.

In the case of the car collision it goes into damaging the car, and hopefully to a lesser extent, the occupants of the vehicle.

In the case of the football player, some of the

energy is absorbed into the padding, but when the energy overcomes the ability of the padding to absorb energy it is expended into the human body. Sometimes that results in a bruise, sore muscle, but other times the energy dissipation can be more damaging.

How do we know how much kinetic energy is in a collision? If we don't know how much energy to expect, we can't possibly figure what type of protective gear we need to prevent injury.

The answer is all in the math.

Kinetic Energy is determined with a simple bit of multiplication. We simply multiply one-half times the mass times the square of the velocity.

$$KE = \tfrac{1}{2} m v^2$$

As we can see, how fast a mass is moving matters more than anything else when looking for what causes there to be more energy involved. If you want the most energy have a heavy object moving really fast, which is why if you were hit by a fully loaded 18-wheel truck it isn't a good thing. This equation is the physics behind why kickoffs are so dangerous (more on that in later chapters).

Now, remember that brain floating around

inside the skull scenario we were describing. Yes, there is a fluid, which does offer some cushion or "braking" if you want to think of it from that perspective. That is slightly more protective than just having a free-floating in air situation, like a human in a car without a seat belt or airbag. However, the fluid only slows things down, it doesn't stop them, and it certainly doesn't make the risk of injury disappear. To take the risk of injury to zero, we must make the energy go to zero. We can't remove all the mass; therefore, we have to remove the velocity.

The fact is that on every hit, every single one, the brain is going to move around inside the cranium, and for at least one person on the field it is likely to come to an abrupt stop. For that player, when it finally comes to rest it is possible that it may do so because it hit something hard, which as we now know is skull bone, and that stuff is hard.

Ok, I know what you are saying that's it, fully stop playing and watching this barbaric ritual, we can all agree that there should be no more football. Just ban the whole thing now, and all the world will be a safer place, and while we are at it, why don't we wrap all kids in bubble wrap until they are teenagers.

Wait a minute.

Let's not be too hasty.

There are ways to add more "brakes" to the system and gradually slow that hit more over time, just like gradually rather than abruptly braking a car. There are helmets, pads, and other types of gear that have been developed over the years. What is needed is a type of padding that more effectively slows that hit into a roll instead of a jolt. More attention should be given to helmet designs (and in some cases is) that will add structural components to the overall design that will offer a reduction in the g-forces imparted into the head by sending that kinetic energy some other place.

That is correct, it is possible to give the energy someplace else to go. That is how Kevlar works to protect the wearer from a bullet, it spreads the force out over a larger area. It can't be said often enough, the energy is going to go someplace, and with intelligent design work we can be the ones that determine where it stops.

How do Concussions Happen in American Football

Let's review how a concussion might occur on the football field step by step:

1) The Quarterback gets the ball from the center and the play begins according to a plan (hopefully).

2) A player on the defensive squad finds the player who has the ball (maybe the QB, maybe someone else by that point).

3) A tackle occurs.

4) The person(s) involved in the tackle have a series of external forces slowing their body rapidly, this could be each other and this could be the earth (or artificial turf, more on that whole mess later).

5) The brain is in motion, and that is going to come to a halt in short order.

6) The brain stops moving at a slightly different time than the body, which turns out to be a little bit later than the skull stops moving because it is meeting resistance caused by the fluid (among other reasons), and the brain isn't all that happy about it.

7) Repeat this process…a lot.

The harder those hits, either into the ground or into the other player, the higher the chance for a concussion and the more severe that injury is when it happens. This is especially true when these hits are repeated as frequently as they are during the playing season (recall that discussion of second injuries being easier to receive). There are even arguments, that have some legitimacy, that say even micro-concussions, which might be difficult to diagnose or even be below the threshold for possible detection of most medical scanning equipment, are what occurs in football more often than anything else. It is also possible that a large number of micro-concussions is far more dangerous than previously considered for the longer term health of those engaged in the game.

There is a well written book (with movie adaptation) called *Truth Doesn't have a Side*, by Dr. Bennet Omalu. While this book did show the dangers of concussions it never got into what might be done to prevent them (other than not paying the game). It also spent a lot of time discussing the life of the author, which while interesting, isn't our goal in this book. We want to get to an understanding of the potential dangers and show a pathway to solving those problems. Sometimes that will be rule changes, sometimes that will be treatment, other times it is equipment. But, these problems can be solved one at a time until the game is both safe and enjoyable to watch.

How is a Concussion Treated?

Let's assume someone, athlete or not, has suffered a concussive blow to the head.

What comes next?

In general, medical treatment for someone diagnosed with a concussion is a relatively cookie cutter process. In other words, most patients are treated essentially the same depending on the severity of the injury.

That is staggering to us, but we will explain that in a minute. First, let's take a look at the typical process, treatment regimen, or suggestions doctors give for a patient recovering from this type of injury.

The doctor will first and foremost recommend that the patient rest. This isn't just rest for the body, this will include instructions to rest the brain. Basically, the patient will be told to no do things that make them think too much. This is both physical and mental "nap time."

Let's put that in some sort of football terminology.

If you are playing the NFL level you are the exception among people playing the sport, not the rule. Most players are not ever going to reach that level (sorry to break it to everyone, some will make it but many do not). Therefore, if you suffered a concussion playing football, with a high degree of likelihood you are a student. So, for the sake of discussion, let's think about a guy playing for a large, well known University like Notre Dame. Then let's go ahead and tell that junior at a highly competitive University that they can't use their brain for a few days. That sort of thing is not going to help his future as it will impact his abilities as a student, but it will help his brain. Therefore, I think it is easy to see the strong motivation to find ways to limit this type of injury at all levels of the sport, not just at the professional level which gets all the news coverage.

As an additional step many doctors, when it comes to their patients, will suggest shortened work day or school days. Has anyone ever had a professor who would be ok with that? Neither of us can remember one either.

Eventually, the signs and symptoms will reduce in severity, and hopefully disappear (depending on the severity of the injury).

However, during recovery when the patient is still suffering from pain symptoms resulting from their concussion, typically this will be treated with some type of pain reliever. A dose of acetaminophen (Tylenol is an example) is suggested and ibuprofen is to be avoided. In other words, here go take this little pain management pill, that over the counter thing you take when you have had a long day or too much to drink the night before.

That's it for the pain management aspect of injury recovery. There isn't anything groundbreaking here. Rest and take some pain reliever. In other words, walk it off, maybe drink some water.

There are organizations researching new types of treatments out there, and we wish them well. We hope they succeed, but for the moment the widely accepted treatment is as we described.

Earlier in this section there was a brief mention that we were flabbergasted by the way that these injuries are treated in a cookie cutter fashion. Having been around enough concussions and concussed people we, and most neurologists, will tell you that no two brains are the same. To be more specific, no two brain *injuries* are the same. Even if the MRIs done on two individual patients are compared and a virtually identical injury is seen, there will be differences in the patient and their manifestations of symptoms, not to mention recovery process required to get things back to normal.

The two-step treatment of rest and pain management for everyone isn't all that well tailored to help specific patients recover quickly. What is necessary is a more customized approach that can be developed for each patient on an individual, case by case basis.

Now, are we going to suggest what should be done?

What should a treatment protocol look like?

Not at all, neither of us are medical professionals, but every single doctor we have spoken to has uniformly agreed that there must be a better way. There is current research being conducted on finding that better method, and we hope those researchers can develop that process quickly. The ideas and concepts we have heard, and methods to deal with a concussion that are being researched are a bit out of the box, but we are by no means recommending these to anyone in particular. That is for the individual patient and their doctor to determine.

As we said, some medical groups are starting to look at ways to treat the whole patient. This would be a treatment regimen where the brain injury is tailored specifically to the patient rather than just following a recipe that consists of performing step one, then step two, repeat as needed. That might work perfectly for the directions on shampoo, but they shouldn't be how we treat someone with a brain injury.

Those groups doing a more in-depth analysis and treatment program where they do customize treatment processes for each patient are finding that doing so results in a reduced return to work time (meaning faster recovery) and fewer long-term impacts. We know this type of result becomes the goal of all treatment programs, but we hope that a tailored to the patient treatment regime becomes the norm rather than the exception. This is far beyond the scope of this book, and assuming they make progress may become a topic for a book in the future.

A Concussion Protocol for the Game

The NFL is always changing, or at least attempting to evolve so that the sport is more enjoyable to watch and safer to play. Attempting to improve the Concussion Protocol is part of that evolution of the game that is going on currently.

Changes at the NFL level typically drive changes at the NCAA level and below. While it might be instructive to discuss what the official protocol is right now, it would become dated very quickly as it would likely change before this book goes to print. That should tell everyone how seriously the league is taking the concussion situation. They aren't looking at what they are doing as "good enough," they are looking at it like "here is what we are doing, what else can we do to continue to improve." While we won't discuss *the* protocol, we will give a detailed example of *a* protocol (and, honestly this is largely based on the NFL protocol at the time we wrote this).

Whenever you try to accomplish anything complicated in life, it is best to have a plan. In this case, our goal is to develop a plan to limit concussions in contact sports, particularly American style Football.

Define that plan however you want, but with a sport that includes as much physical contact as American Football or even Hockey a plan must be written down, agreed upon and executed. This allows the best opportunity to have any kind of positive and consistent widespread positive impact on player safety.

This plan should be (and ours was) put together as a result of input from medical as well as sports experts and those persons must be familiar with head trauma. The medical professionals from the treatment side, and the sports experts (likely former players at the highest level) must be familiar with where, when and how head injuries are most likely to occur on the playing field. Otherwise, the plan isn't going to be as effective as it otherwise could be in solving the problem. In addition to all of that, those who control the plan must be ready to change that plan when a better one comes along, which will mostly likely be because there is new information obtained as a result of the new plan protocols just put into place.

As a famous Texan, and huge football fan, T. Boone Pickens, once said, "A fool with a plan will beat a genius with no plan." No one wants to be a fool with no plan, and not everyone can be a genius. Now, before anyone jumps to some conclusion concerning our opinion of how smart the people in charge of the NFL concussion protocol are, or are not, there are smart people working for the league, and they have a plan. Let's hope they continue to evaluate that plan and improve it whenever, and however possible.

To their credit, the NFL has tweaked, and shows every indication that they will continue to tweak their concussion protocol to improve the situation. As you will see in the player interviews later in this book, many of the players agree things are greatly improved over what they were just a few decades ago. We are certain that the organizing bodies at all levels of the sport will continue to look for ways to improve player safety.

The first steps in any concussion protocol must start before the season begins. Players, managers, coaches, and other sideline personnel must be trained (or have some refresher training) on how to identify the signs and symptoms that may be present in someone who has suffered a concussion. It isn't one person's job or another to identify these injuries, this is for everyone to determine. If someone, anyone on the field, notices something not right with a player they must speak up. Teammates know each other, they know how the people they play with walk, talk, and respond to various situations. If someone isn't responding as usual it is imperative that they speak up, that they not be shy because that other person's brain health is on the line. Being wrong and the identified player doesn't have a concussion might take them out of the game for a play or two while medical personnel take a closer look, being right could save them from a lifelong debilitating injury.

Why is it important to speak up as soon as possible?

In any concussive injury there is a time period referred to as "the golden hour." What that means in layperson terms is getting a concussive injury treated sooner, rather than later is vital to long-term recovery chances, and speeds the time to recovery (especially in more severe cases).

Even before the season begins players should have a physical exam. This already happens all the way down to high school. Right now, this is a standard physical exam, something comparable to the standard annual physical exam with a family physician for someone who isn't an athlete. That could be modified a bit, given the current focus on brain injuries. Part of that exam could, and perhaps should, be a neurophysiological test.

These sorts of tests will give a baseline for someone's brain health at a time when they aren't injured. The data obtained in such a test could come in very handy as a baseline for during the season if a potential concussive injury occurs. Some of these injuries can be minor, almost undetectable in nature. One way to make diagnosis easier, and more certain, is to have a such a baseline for comparison from the individual who suffered the potential injury. It is always best to know how something functions when it isn't injured (or damaged).

Now that we have worked our way through preseason, let's focus on game day. The NFL recently made an addition to the concussion protocol that seems like a good idea.

During the 2018-2019 season, each team was assigned an Unaffiliated Neurotrauma Consultant (UNC). This person is a medical doctor who is impartial, and independent of any team (as in not a fan, if that's possible). He must be board certified, or at least eligible in neurology, neurological surgery, or emergency medicine with documented experience in head injuries. This person's job is to identify any warning signs of a concussion when examining a player, as well as any potential hits that might be something that could have yielded a concussion in order to request an examination for a player who may not realize they were concussed. These people will be at every game and will observe any sideline concussion assessments that are performed on any player on their assigned team.

Long term this could be an interesting change and has the potential to massively increase player safety as pertains to concussive injuries. We believe this step is likely to have a positive effect on long-term brain health. Fingers crossed that this is a positive change. During this most recent season (2018-2019) the treatment of concussed (or potentially concussed) players was seemingly improved. It will take several seasons before we know for certain what kind of positive impact these changes will have.

Another new addition at the professional level is that there will be two certified athletic trainers assigned to the stadium booth, with access to multiple video feeds, and instant replay capabilities to aid in the recognition of a potentially concussive hit. When these spotters observe a player whom is unstable, or displays concussion signs they will contact the team physician immediately and ensure an evaluation of that individual is undertaken immediately.

In other words, the league has realized that given the size of players, and the speed now achieved on the field thanks to modern training techniques, to solve this problem will require more than just players watching players. They are determined to have as many eyes as possible on the problem.

In addition to eyes watching, during a game, if any player exhibits a loss of consciousness, confusion or amnesia, that player should head to the sidelines for an evaluation. Some of these may be self-reported, others may be reported by teammates. This is crucial as while a concussion patient may not have a visible injury, these are not normal behaviors and are likely the result of too much kinetic energy not finding anywhere but the head to call its final resting place.

As a next step in our concussion protocol, if a sideline assessment confirms that a player is at risk, or can't be cleared as being concussion free, a more comprehensive locker room assessment should be performed. This is highly dependent upon the level of the sport as NFL stadiums have more medical equipment available than local high schools. If any doubt is shown in the locker room the player should be elevated to the next level of medical care available.

If the locker room assessment couldn't clear a player, that last paragraph likely resulted in a trip to the local hospital. How likely are they to return to the next week's game? Well, there is no single, guaranteed answer to that question that will apply to every player and every injury as everyone's brain health and brain health history are different. That is a decision for the player, the doctor, and the coach. Football is a team sport, and a team is needed to solve this problem. If the organizations, both athletic and medical at all levels can put their collective experience to work, perhaps concussions will no longer be a major concern in American Football.

Is this "concussion protocol" the way the NFL or NCAA has always operated?

Hell no.

Jay has reminded Tim, on many occasions that when he played if you "got your bell rung," and felt a little fuzzy in the head you were told to tape an aspirin to your helmet and get your ass back out there.

That was the league of the 1970s and 1980s, it isn't the league of today. Tomorrow's league will be better and safer than what we have right now.

Should the calls for banning the sport be adhered to?

Of course not.

There was a time in history when a President of the United States considered banning the sport from coast to coast. We bet you didn't know that. More on that bit of trivia later, but it was as a result of safety concerns.

Changes were made at that time, and the game became safer and is still part of our society.

Can there be additional changes that make it safer than it is today?

Absolutely, we improved before and we can improve again.

Is it safe to let children play the game? We believe so (past a certain age when it comes to the tackle version of the sport).

Where do we go From Here?

So far in this book, we have discussed what a concussion is, we have even outlined a protocol, or process to deal with them when one occurs while playing Football.

Where do we go from here?

Next, we will give a brief history of the sport, and we think you will agree it is much safer now than it has been at various points in the past. Not many people ever think about the history of the sport prior to the day they became a fan. Sure, people have seen the pictures of leather helmets, but do you really consider what it was like to play the sport back then versus today? The players were slower, but the rules weren't as protective of players either.

Also, American Football is much older than people tend to believe, and the safety aspects are shockingly different now than they were when the sport was born. They were largely non-existent at one point.

Next, we will discuss how the sport is played, what the different player positions are and how the physics of those plays might be understood better to design safety equipment specific to each position. Most of this will be review for fans of the game, but we want this book to be for anyone considering becoming involved, or for those who aren't familiar with the details of the sport to be left out of the discussion. Then we want to describe the current game versus the original game and go through the steps of how we got from where it all began to where we are today.

After that we will look at all aspects of how to prevent this injury. This will include training, hydration, techniques, procedures, and yes safety equipment.

We have a few interviews with some people who have been some trainers who have helped get people ready to play at the professional level. This will allow a deeper understanding of the societal perception of what is going on today, and how it might impact the future of the sport than might be achieved from just two guys' perspectives.

Finally, we will have a discussion of the future. What can we change, how can we change it and how might it help make the sport we have come to love something future generations can continue to enjoy, without fear if they permit their children to participate that they may suffer some lifelong brain injury.

As a final introductory note, we want to say that we do offer some potential solutions in this book. These are merely offered to get people to start to think out of the box. We are not saying one solution, or another will be the silver bullet that solves head injuries forever. Some combination of these will help, and there are likely many other things we haven't thought of. The important part of this discussion is that people start to think, make changes, and solve this problem.

It will not be easy or quick to solve, it will take time and considerable effort. While simply banning the sport is the easy way out, we don't feel it is the right thing to do, and not the foundations upon which a free society should operate. We solve problems, we don't ban things. We come together to solve big problems, and this is one that we can clearly fix by putting smart people to task at finding the right set of steps to get to a safer, more enjoyable football game. This is not a solution that will magically appear overnight, it is going to take time but it can be done.

If I can access any website in the world from the tiny battery powered device in my pocket, we can certainly solve this problem caused by simple collisions.

Chapter 2
A History of American Football

In order to fully understand a sport, or how that sport can be played safely, we must really understand what that sport is. We must understand how it is played, what the various player positions are, and where it all came from.

Why?

A smart person once said those who fail to understand their history are destined to repeat it. If injuries were once worse than they are today, might we be making things worse if we alter a modern rule and without realizing it, put things back to how they were?

Which is why we do our homework, even when we don't want to.

Many people may share the belief that the sport of football didn't really get started in a modern sense until Tom Brady was elevated to be the starting quarterback for the New England Patriots. Following this meteoric rise, he then went on to have more Super Bowl appearances than almost any other player in the history of the league, but that isn't really the case. Football really started long before then.

It got started long before television was even a

household thing, and a very long time before football was so dominant in the ratings battles on those magic picture boxes that we all have hanging on our walls.

It didn't magically appear today in the current form for our viewing pleasure. Many people came along throughout the ages to make rule changes, introduce new equipment, modernize the entertainment aspects of the sport, long before what we watch today to organize the first game. It did not just spring forward on a Sunday afternoon when a few guys got together and figured out a set of rules on a bar napkin. The sport found its roots in a combination of Rugby-style Football as well as what was then referred to as Association Football.

It is important to take a moment to recall what those two sports are and how they are played, just in case you aren't familiar with them. We also need to see just how far back these things go in history to understand if banning them would ever be impactful. Banning something new might be possible, banning something that is ingrained in our culture deeply for a long period of time is a lot more difficult.

Rugby is by no means new to humankind, it originated way back with the Greeks and Romans. These early nations are known to have played a great number of sports, they were as competitive as can be imagined. Many of those sports involved a ball of some kind. Some of these ancient athletic events involved extensive use of the feet to move a ball from one place to another. This is a bit of a departure from modern American Football in which the hands are used extensively, but these were the early days.

There was also a Roman game called Harpastum which was probably adapted from the Greek team sport known as Episkyros. The last sport is so old that the first known evidence of it was found in a manuscript written by a Greek playwright somewhere around 350 B.C, meaning by that point in history it was popular enough to have plays (the modern equivalent being movies) written about it.

The description of how the game unfolded in that play (once translated appropriately to English) resembles modern day Rugby. To say that Rugby, and its more modern derivative American Football, are ingrained in our culture is accurate. Based on these dates, it has certainly been around in one form or another for a very long time.

Anyone still think it can just be banned by some group of politicians and it will go away instantly and forever?

When was the last time a group of politicians told a large group of people to stop doing something their words actually achieve the goal of the activity coming to a halt?

Did it work at all when they tried to ban alcohol? Pass a beer and tell me that story.

In a modern sense, Rugby is a sport in which a ball that physically speaking closely resembles the ball used in American football (see photo).

While playing Rugby the ball can be kicked, carried or passed from player to player. Teams score points by getting the ball across an opponent's goal line or by kicking it between two goal posts. In this way, it is indeed a lot like modern football. Sure, there are fewer pads, no helmets, and plays start much differently, but there are obvious similarities.

One immediately noticeable difference is that instead of a line of scrimmage, there is a scrum. A scrum involves players standing closely together bent over with their heads down in an attempt to gain possession of the ball. Once the ball is in play, and a player has the ball and has somehow escape the terror circle of the scrum, they can be tackled by the opposing team, thus stopping forward progress.

We could write, and there are, books about

Rugby. This isn't one of them, but the main point we wanted to get across is that the two sports are closely related, and ancient. However, our focus is on American Football. We wanted to mention Rugby in order to demonstrate that football isn't just an American invention, and it is by no means new. It has been embedded in the psyche of human beings in one form or another for more than 2,000 years, which is longer than Christianity and multiple other organized religions. Now football isn't a religion, but it has been around a very long time indeed.

Still think a simple ban with some politicians in business suits signing a piece of paper is going to make this whole thing just go away?

Not a chance.

Wait, that's not all.

The other sport that had an immediate influence on American Football's development over the years was originally referred to as Association Football but is now known simply as soccer. While soccer (Football to most of the word) doesn't have tackling or passes thrown through the air by a guy protected by an offensive line, it is similar in some ways.

Players still form teams, there are offensive as well as defensive techniques, strategies, and even a goal line. While it may be a minimal contact sport compared to the American version of Football, one can't help but notice the influence. It was more noticeable in the style of football played here in the United States a century ago (discussed later in this chapter), but that influence can be seen if the evolution of the modern game is known.

Hold on to your socks, you are about to learn about that evolution!

If we consider that both Rugby and Soccer had a direct influence on the American version of Football one can't help but understand the immediate attraction it holds to all types of sports fans. If you like Rugby, football has something for you. If you like Soccer, ditto. It has a widespread mass appeal that has pushed it to become the phenomenon that it is today. It is a phenomenon that has started to spread outside the United States and may soon become just as much of a worldwide sports spectacular.

It doesn't matter if you are a fan of the aerobic tradition and grace that can be found while watching soccer, or the more impact-oriented action of rugby, football has something to offer.

It may be partially because of the ability of the game and organizing bodies to evolve over the years to suit modern athletes and audiences. The organizers were even smart enough to evolve the field so that it would become more appealing on television, which was probably the smartest move they ever made.

When did we the American version of the sport first appear?

Who took the time to organize everything, and when were these two very different sports combined, in a more formal sense?

Somewhere in the late 1800s.

Exactly when depends upon who you talk to.

It is generally agreed upon that in the late 1860s things became more formal, and prior to that it was more accurately described as a bunch of guys messing around in a field. However, one thing that known for certain is that there was a game on November 6, 1869 played between Rutgers and Princeton Universities that is considered to be the kickoff (pardon the pun, we couldn't pass up the opportunity) of the sport.

Was it exactly the same as the game we know today?

Nope, not even close.

First, at this point in history football was still played with a round ball, closely resembling a soccer ball (see photograph).

That isn't the only departure from the modern

sport.

There were 25 players on each team. The ball could not be picked up or carried (much like gameplay during soccer today). It could be kicked or batted with your hands, feet, head, shins, stomach, whatever you wanted, just not carried. The intent of the team on offense was to get that thing across the goal line, at any cost.

Sounds a lot like soccer, only with tackling, which honestly, might make soccer more exciting.

For the moment we will just let the soccer hooligans up in the stands feed our desire for tackling. Maybe the lack of tackling in the sport is why soccer has hooligans and for the most part football does not. Humans do seem to enjoy watching violence (see MMA, boxing, hockey, every traffic accident with people slowing down to see the blood should it exist).

For many years this new combined sport remained a game played between universities and lacked an extensive set of formal rules for many years. The basic agreement was that the rules of the match would be whatever the host school decided. This made the rules a bit different from school to school and made preparing for a game difficult. In other words, it was not the best-organized thing in the world. The challenges involved in prepping to play a particular team made games disjointed in many ways, but it was fun to watch, and the fan base grew.

The first formalization of the rules occurred in October of 1873 at a meeting when Yale, Columbia, Princeton and Rutgers Universities all agreed to have representatives get together and agree upon a standard set of rules for all schools to use. That certainly make practicing and preparation for a specific opponent far easier, not to mention officiating more predictable.

At that meeting things started, in some ways, to shift towards the game we have today. They decided that teams would consist of 20 players, and fields would be 400 feet long by 250 feet wide in size.

It wasn't a huge leap forward, but it was a start.

It was a successful meeting in that something was decided (if you ever work for a large company you will get that joke and find it funny), but there was a problem. One of the major players of the sport was not in attendance. Harvard decided to sit the meeting out as they preferred a more rugby-like approach to the game versus the rules preferred by everyone else. Their main desire was to ensure that players could use their hands to carry the ball, at least for games in which they participated in, would be permitted.

Harvard got what they wanted.

Once the new rules were agreed upon, the first formal league game played with the now official, more Harvard style rules was in 1875 between Harvard and Yale. Once this transition to the uniformed rules of game play occurred, students at the various universities known to be involved in the game all agreed they, like the fans, enjoyed this version better than the "no hands" approach. This led to the officially formation of the Intercollegiate Football Association. Shortly after that league formation, the number of players was reduced to 11 players on the field at once per team, and they instituted the snap to start the play that we see in the game today, thereby eliminating any use of the scrum used in Rugby.

Today, just as in several points in history, American Football faces a turning point. There are those that say it should be banned. There are some that say the league should be stripped of every advantage it has from tax breaks to public financing of stadiums, and while the current league is on the way out the door it should pay a financial fine so large that it would only be referred to as the fine of the millennium, intended to strip the owners of their personal wealth because, after all, they knew something about the concussion problem long ago and didn't do anything about it so they could continue to profit.

As we shall see in future chapters, as we already have in this one, the sport has and will continue to evolve. As a society, we will make football safer, as has been done in the past. If we look at our history, and the length of time the sport has been around in one form or another we will watch the game, or something similar for as long as anyone reading this is alive. It is here to stay, and no attempt to ban will be successful at anything more than creating nationwide massive protest rallies in which politicians will not be welcome parties.

What else is different today than it was in these earliest days? What other evolutions have already happened?

Well, back then there was almost no protective equipment worn by players, at least not any officially required gear. Some players got creative, stuffing padding in their pants or shirts, but there was no requirement of any kind. That certainly has changed for the better and will continue to improve.

The addition of the snap had some strange, unexpected, and unintentional impacts on the game. In Rugby, a team with bad field position after a scrum tends to punt. That was until the Princeton team came up with a new strategy, they wanted to take advantage of the situation created by this change. The snap, unlike the scrum, meant that possession of the ball was uncontested. You knew who would get the ball, and where the play would start. Princeton figured out that if they were in the lead it was possible to just hold the ball forever, basically just hold position, stand around and let game clock run to zero. This would prevent the opposing team from scoring at all. This worked pretty well if you were in the lead and managed to gain possession of the football.

Great idea if you are the coach trying to maintain a winning record. Not all that interesting if you are a fan who bought a ticket and spent your afternoon off from work in the stands.

This became a common, although boring practice of the game. That was until this tactic was carried to an illogical extreme in a few crazy games.

In 1881 there was a game between Yale and Princeton. They both were undefeated and badly wanted to remain so. The two coaches decided to use the tactic of holding the ball with no attempt to advance, for an entire half of the game each. This resulted in a zero-zero tie.

Let's just say the spectators hated this, it was boring. In a modern sense, it would have made for horrible television. This type of behavior is something that the league would never allow because of the television ratings dip it would cause. Thus, there was an evolution of the rules.

The sport was facing a crisis, and to prevent this style of game from becoming the norm, several things were considered.

A man named Walter Camp took charge of the situation. This is a man who has come to be known as the "Father of American Football," but at the time was the captain of Yale's team, and he proposed a rule change to improve the situation.

In 1882 it was decided that each team had three downs to advance the ball five yards and failing to get those yards resulted in a turnover of possession to the other team (no punt was involved at the time). Wouldn't that be an interesting twist to the modern game? Allow the four downs, keep the line at ten yards, but no more punting. You must try at all costs to get those ten yards.

I wonder what the NFL Commissioner's office would say about that one? Anyone know someone in that office? Maybe we should make a call.

A team going for it on fourth down is always exciting and that would certainly happen more often than it does currently. It would likely increase the scores of every game ever played due to field positions on turnover.

In addition to making the games more exciting, this change made a few things happen. For instance, Rugby and American Football were now distinctly different sports.

The second was that the appearance of the field was changed a bit. The five-yard line marks were added to the playing surface, and remain there today, this was done to aid in measuring distances the ball has moved. As a result, the field now resembles a gridiron, and as a direct result of these lines, the nickname frequently used by sports announcers was born.

There was another change to the field that was enacted at this point. The physical dimensions were altered. The playing surface was reduced to 110 by 53.333 yards.

Next up for tuning was the scoring system that gave four points for a touchdown, two for a safety, which is what we would now call the extra point, and five for a field goal. They also legalized tackling below the waist.

The final innovation that made the separation from Rugby to this totally new sport was the legalization of blocking. Blocking would be called interference in Rugby and is illegal in that sport, but the activity is highly encouraged in football.

All these new rules were designed to make the game distinctive from the others, not to mention more exciting, and in some ways safer than it had been before. However, despite these new rules, some of which put a focus on player safety, football was still considered a dangerous sport.

There was another problem with fans and players finding any kind of consistency game to game. The rules were starting to be formalized but in many ways they were still very loose, and *safety was not the primary concern* of the teams involved. It might be more accurate to say that safety was barely a thought.

Dangerous play formations were commonplace. One formation, called the flying wedge, was particularly common and broke more bones than just about any other play ever seen on the field. In fact, formations like the wedge would not only result in serious injuries but were directly responsible for more than one death.

That is correct, that wasn't a misprint. People used to die as a direct result of injuries sustained while playing football.

The year 1905 was the peak of fatalities. *In that year 19 fatalities could directly be attributed to on-field activities nationwide.* Now, in the modern world, we occasionally see people call for congressional inquiry or investigations and they will say things along the line of "oh these modern politicians just want to get their faces on television." Politicians and football have been involved with one another before. That particularly vicious 1905 season resulted in a threat by President Theodore Roosevelt to abolish the game forever (how that would be enforced is anyone's guess) unless serious changes were made.

After this threat by a, let's just say well-known politician, no fewer than sixty-two colleges and universities who had active teams participating in intercollegiate games sent representatives to meet in New York City to discuss immediate changes. These proceedings resulted in some new rules, almost all aimed at player safety.

The outcome of this wasn't just to fix the crisis in front of them. They accomplished a little bit more than that, which pushed the game to grow in popularity. But they also managed to formalize the game more than ever before.

The formation of what we refer to today as the National Collegiate Athletic Association (NCAA) was one notable result. The concept of the NCAA is that it would be an official organization with the power to make any changes to the rules governing the game in the future for Universities.

The NCAA wanted (and still desires) a league

that can evolve when needed. Learning and improving is what life and sports is all about. The moment something stops changing for the better is the moment you can almost be certain that it is on the decline and may cease to exist. As no system, league, or organization is ever perfect.

Some of the gameplay still being practiced at this point might seem odd to modern fans. This evolution of the game into a modern form, when it was already popular, demonstrates just how far the sport has come. It also teaches us that changes can be positive and how change should not be feared but embraced. If a change turns out to not be for the better, there is nothing in the world wrong with changing things back to the way they were.

Now as we hope you will agree, obviously we need to learn from the past, and our little history lesson is not yet complete (but close).

Prior to 1906 any form of the forward pass was not allowed and allowing this type of play to become legal was met with skepticism. Just as some of the proposed changes of today are being met with skepticism. Despite the public doubt this forward pass change has obviously stuck around and become embraced by players and fans. It took a while for this change to really catch on, and Football didn't instantly become the passing game of today. This change was limited in use for a time and there were some restrictions on its use in the rules, but that would eventually change, and in the league today the forward pass is what many teams build the majority of their offensive strategy around.

During that same period in history, other rules were altered. The time limit of the game was reduced from seventy to the sixty minutes used today. The distance needed for a first down was changed from five to the ten yards. There are probably some offensive squads out there today wishing it was still five yards, but the rule change has stuck around. It has caused the game to become far more dramatic in ways.

In 1909 field goals were reduced to three points from five. Then in 1912 touchdowns were raised to the six points currently in the rule book.

The evolution didn't slow down. By 1918 a few more changes had firmly taken hold. The field was reduced to one hundred yards from goal line to goal line, but the end zones were added and defined to be ten yards each. The number of downs was changed to the four and given that a team must go ten yards instead of the original five, this was very much needed as first downs would have become far less common, and overall game scoring had reduced.

Two other important additions round out the

rapid evolution that was rolling along. The roughing the passer rule was added (and later updated), and eligible pass receivers were now permitted to catch a pass anywhere on the field. The last one impacting the receivers catching a passed ball eliminated a rule that was challenging to enforce and made the game more playable.

In the modern game, there are a few changes that are being discussed, some of them are likely going to be very hard to enforce, so we shall see if they stick around or are modified as was the case with passing rules.

This rounds out the changes and what is now considered the modern game was born (we wanted to say kicked off, but we adopted a one obvious pun per book rule). There have been more shifts that were largely minor by comparison that have happened over the years, and we will talk about the transition to television later which has created the financially successful league of today, but as for rules to the game these are the main points that have been put in place to form the modern league.

One last important bit of trivia before we move on from this history lesson.

Where did the concept of paying people to play come from?

Seriously, it is a game, why should anyone get

paid to play a game?

We hope you can sense the sarcasm in that question.

Well, certainly even back then, there were fans, tickets, vendors, and other people around making a few bucks every time two of the major teams went head to head. The players just showed up for fun, probably for some for notoriety, or some college spirit to represent their school as athletes. There were teams that played outside of college, and it was becoming a more common thing for lots of towns to have "representation" against another town's team, but things weren't at the level of the well-organized league of today where the organizing body decides which cities have teams, much less determines who plays when and where.

The earliest record of someone getting paid (officially) was in 1892. That talented person was a man by the name of William "Pudge" Heffelinger. He was paid $500…in 1892!!! He received this hefty sum for his participation in a single game, way back then. Adjusting for the value of money over time that is the equivalent of roughly $12,500 today. Not a bad single game payday for the first guy to ever get paid to play the sport.

For the record, the team that paid him was from Allegheny Pennsylvania and the game was against a team from Pittsburgh. For point of comparison this was 17 years before the Wright Brothers took flight, so teams tended to be geographically close to one another if they were going to play, otherwise organizing a game would be prohibitively expensive due to transportation costs, not to mention time to travel from game to game.

Before this time no real direct cash payments were given, but teams would help players find jobs and others gave out things like watches that many of the players would sell off for a few dollars. The only other perk that players had was that they, mostly, would be reimbursed for their expenses.

Eventually paying players became the norm at the professional level, salaries went up, leagues were formed, and the NFL was born. The league we know today was officially formed in 1920 as the American Professional Football Association (the name change would come later), and by 1922 was solidly the official body for the organization and officiation of the sport at the highest level.

The NFL is still, without a doubt, in the driver's seat of American Football to this day.

Chapter 3
Team Composition

We live in a strange world. The advent of social media, 24/7 world news, multiple cable stations specializing in sporting events as well as talk shows about those sporting events, and we wouldn't want to leave out internet blogs have worked together to turn the world into a place where everyone's opinion can be heard. Some people tend to render that opinion without any real understanding of the subject matter being discussed, but why should that stop anyone.

Therefore, we wanted to take moment away from the core conversation to define who these guys running around the field are. It is also important to understand why they are doing particular things and the typical risks involved in various positions under normal gameplay. We want these definitions to be legitimate and not a matter of poorly researched opinion. That way we can enter a substantive meaningful discussion of how to many the game safer for people at various positions.

Breakdown of a Team

For those that have a long-term history with the

game this chapter may not be necessary. For anyone who isn't a long-term fan, or perhaps has just a passing interest in the game, or maybe even none at all, but have been following the concussion crisis, this chapter will be helpful. We also hope to be able to inform parents who are attempting to decide if they should permit their child to participate in youth football, we hope to break down the positions various players are in, and explain which positions run risks of which types of injuries.

An American Football team is broken down into three main subcomponents or squads. These are the offense, defense, and special teams.

During gameplay the offensive and defensive players line up directly across from one another before the start of every down. This area between the two main bodies of players is known as the line of scrimmage. There is a small space in between the two lines that has become known as the "neutral zone." However, anyone who has watched football understands that very little in the game is neutral. It is indeed a game of ground control. You control that ground by being better, bigger, meaner, faster, more violent, having a better strategy, not to mention athletic ability than your opponent. The team who does a better job of controlling the ground will win.

Offense

The primary job of the offense can be described in two ways. First, and most obvious is to score points. Second is to control the game clock and prevent the other team from getting the ball for extended periods of time. An offense needs to master controlling the clock, so they can prevent the opposing team from having any scoring opportunities. This is a bit trickier since they modified the rules with a delay of game clock, but it is still an important strategy.

The offense can be broken down a bit further into specific positions with certain areas of responsibility, and talents.

There are linemen and a group of guys behind them on the field, all of whom have pre-defined roles and responsibilities. We will describe all of that in a second, but for the moment there is one important thing to understand. There is a rule that states that seven offensive players must be on the line of scrimmage before every play, and there can be no more than four players behind it. That makes the offense (and defense) consist of eleven people on the field at once.

Quarterback

This is the guy we all know. He is the one

credited with victories and blamed for the defeats more often than anyone else on the field.

He is the guy that the coaches communicate play choices to; he informs the rest of the offense what to do, and how to do it. If he spots something once the offensive squad forms up on the line of scrimmage, he is also the guy who makes the change to the upcoming play on the fly by calling an audible. In short, he is the defacto on-field leader of the offense, and the one who knows what is going on as well as, if not better than the head coach. Most head coaches would claim they know better, but the quarterback has a slightly different motivation. The defense isn't trying to hurl the coach to the ground with violence of action every sixty seconds, the quarterback has that little bit of motivation to keep his head focused.

Once the ball is snapped, and the play has begun and he has one job, to make sure forward progress is made. He will do this by any means necessary. He may pass the ball, hand it off to a runner, or run like hell himself. I say run like hell himself because if you had ever met an NFL-level defensive player, and that player was behind you, intent on making sure you were thrown to the ground, you would run like hell. I suspect many quarterbacks run a 40-yard dash faster on the field than during any practice or spring training session.

As we said earlier, because of the high visibility of Quarterbacks are generally thought of as the leader on the field. They are also commonly team captains and informally take on a greater level of responsibility than many players both on and off the field. This hasn't always been the case, and there have been captains in other positions.

Make no mistake, off the field matters as much as on the field. Football is a team sport, and these guys spend more time together than some people spend with their families. They need to get along on and off the field, and with football there are a lot of off the field "fan based" activities that take up a lot of time at the professional and college level. These things matter to the sport and aren't likely to change.

That results in these guys not just being athletes. They don't get to just go play their game and go home.

Remember all that 24/7 news coverage we mentioned?

That results in quarterbacks being some of the most scrutinized guys on the field. I don't think in the modern game there is a single NFL level, and in some cases NCAA level quarterback, that can go out to dinner without someone spotting them and trying to grab pictures from across the restaurant or begging for an autograph. In some cases, it may be a slightly different reaction in that someone may throw things at them as they leave that same situation, depending upon how a recent game went, or which team's fan spotted that particular QB.

On the field quarterbacks are a common target. Not because people on the defensive squad don't like them, merely due to the fact that they are common ball handlers. As a result, they can be attacked from any side on virtually any play. The danger to these players is widespread. The potential for concussion is high.

As a small sidenote that has nothing to do specifically with QBs, at times there have been claims that teams were offering "bounties" for "head hunting" of specific players. Now, I know, the term head hunting is just code for getting the guy out of the game, which could easily be a broken leg, but in the modern game with concussion protocols in place a hard hit to the head would do it instantly.

If a quarterback (or any ball carrier) is entered into the concussion protocol, what might have caused that injury? They can come from a variety of places. They can be hit by defensive players causing their head to be whipped from side to side in a whiplash effect, and they can roll back hitting their head on the ground which can also be dangerous. All of these can be with enough force to cause a concussion alone, and on certain tackles, several of these types of potential injuries can happen as a result of a single tackle.

A head-to-head hit is almost impossible to protect against. Most defensive players will try to avoid this as they would be hit just as hard (that pesky equal and opposite force law from physics comes into play here), and in the modern game, this isn't as common as it once was. However, this is also a type of hit that would be very challenging to prevent a concussion should the hit be hard enough. The only method we can see to do so would be improved padding or structural protection mechanisms in helmets of the future.

There are companies out there trying to improve helmets, but it is a hard problem. You can always make a helmet more protective, but that usually means heavier. Currently football helmets are weighing in between 2.5 and 4.5 lbs. That doesn't sound like much, but it puts it close to a full bag of sugar. Take that bag of sugar from your pantry, make sure it is about 1/3 empty and put it on your head for a few hours. See if you think it is "not that bad." Now try to run as fast as you can with that much weight on your head and remember, there are other pads adding additional weight on every player.

Let's look at these physical mechanisms of brain

injury one at a time. To stop the whiplash effect the player's head would have to be stabilized by some type of safety gear.

Is it possible to connect a quarterback's helmet to their shoulder pads in order to provide a great deal of stabilization and still allow them to swivel their head from side to side looking for an open receiver? Some engineers would say yes, others would say maybe, others would disagree completely and say it couldn't be done. Perhaps in the future, this question can be answered by a protective equipment company and this type of threat can be limited in nature by some new kind of protective technology.

The quarterback getting slammed to the ground is something that happens more frequently than players in this position would desire. Several notable Quarterbacks have lost consciousness as a result of a hit on the turf. In a future chapter we will focus on issues with artificial turf and the differences between those installations and natural grass, and how that may (or may not) be a contributing factor into the dangers associated with being tackled as well as the contribution of these types of surfaces to concussions.

Offensive Line

These days it is a cliché saying, but these guys really do have just one job, to protect the ball handler. Simply put, block anyone trying to get past them, sometimes shoving them to the side so a teammate can run out of the backfield and make some forward progress. These are the huge guys in front of the quarterback that rarely, if ever touch the ball. Ok, fine, the center (discussed in a minute) does touch it on every single play, but mostly these guys are not going to be ball carriers in any form, except on a broken play (fumble, etc).

Their job is to hit and get hit often while ensuring that hit is as effective as it would be if the defensive player were hitting a brick wall. This is so that other offensive squad players, who are going to work to move the ball down the field toward the end-zone, remain untouched for longer periods of time than the defense would desire.

Other members of the offense seem to get a ton of press coverage for their concussions, while linemen are rarely discussed at all. We suspect it is because when these other players get hit in a way that could be concussive it is typically more spectacular and has a far greater potential to be seen on the highlight clips from the game which make their way to the nightly sports newscast.

Linemen, unless they make a huge mistake, aren't highlighted. However, they get hit every single play. These may not be concussive hits, but they could be constantly and consistently micro-concussive (small concussions), over and over and over. These repetitive hits may be dangerous to the brain. They aren't fast moving guys (so that velocity part of the equation we discussed doesn't matter as much as the people in some other positions), but they are big and strong.

In order to help these players do their job safely we probably don't need to worry about the turf as they rarely hit the ground as hard as a running back, quarterback or wide receiver. Their helmets, padding, especially the freshness of that padding, does need to be of concern.

Their protective gear is going to be compressed on every single down. What does compression have to do with it you ask?

Think about any time you have a cushiony material. It doesn't matter if it is a pillow or a couch, after the cushion is compressed too often it loses its ability to perform as a cushion. Inside the helmets of every player is a padding designed to protect their head. The linemen will have that padding compressed over and over and over during every game. Refreshing those pads will become necessary very quickly as the first time they get hit and the seventy-first time they are hit their ability to protect the wearer's head is not the same. Some padding companies do better than others, but all degrade over time.

Center

The Center, whose position name derives from the fact that he is, you guessed it, in the center of the offensive line is the player directly in front of the quarterback. He is the one who really puts the play in motion when he snaps the ball to the Quarterback. As a result, he gets a lot of attention from the defensive linemen. Most rational people would want to avoid extra attention from a group of guys that large, and it takes a special person to take on this roll.

This is a position that comes with a lot of responsibility. This player has the best view of what the defensive line is doing, or put another way, what they are planning on doing once the play starts. He looks at how their bodyweight shifts on their heels, where are their eyes focusing, and what is the overall feeling at the line of scrimmage. He can, and often does, make the first line call (telling his teammates what to do) and may call for an overall adjustment of the line positions.

This responsibility makes him one of the on-field leaders. We can think of his position like a Lieutenant to the Quarterback in some ways. In addition to having a leadership role, he has what is possibly one of the most violent positions on the team. He gets hit, and hits someone…hard, on every play. He doesn't just shove someone to the side, he hits the guy or guys in front of him over and over and over again.

After a brief conversation with a retired center we found some interesting things out. The day after a game you will be sore. During the game, you will most likely get a headache. However, if you stay squared with the guy you are going to hit that soreness, and headache is lessened. If you think about skull bones, and other skeletal structures this makes sense. There is a symmetry to the human body, and spreading the force of the hit out evenly, without letting that force bunch up, is helpful. It is also how some armor is designed, with an eye toward spreading the force out evenly over a much larger area.

Back to the job of a center.

Once the ball is in play his job changes to one of blocking whatever defensive player is within his reach. Depending on the play call that the offense is following he may be performing either run or pass blocking, but the operative word is block. His job is to stop someone who wants to get to the ball from getting anywhere close to it, usually with as much violence of action as he can muster within the rules of the game.

In other words, he is a high candidate for a concussion, perhaps not a severe one, but he is a candidate for getting his bell rung multiple times during every game. This is why very specific helmets could (and probably should) be designed for people playing in this position. These helmets should be built to prevent the whiplash problems we discussed earlier.

Given the nature of the job the Center does not need as much head movement range as other positions, and connecting the helmet to the shoulder pads, while still allowing a functional range of motion to be achieved would not be nearly as challenging as it would be for someone playing Quarterback. However, that connection of the helmet to the shoulder pads could be very useful to someone in this position.

Offensive Guard

The two guys on the line of scrimmage to the left and right of the Center are known as the offensive guards. These guys have two jobs depending on the type of play. Their first job is protecting the quarterback, buying him time while he finds an open receiver downfield, and their second job is to open space on the line for the ball carrier to make his way up the field on running plays.

Now, these guys have a job that is almost as violent as the center. Their head is in as much jeopardy as that of the Center but from a slightly different threat. Most Defensive players charge the Center directly from the front. This means the Center mostly moves forwards and backwards, rarely side to side, and therefore most of the threat to his head is from one direction. That makes finding a solution for concussions a little easier. A Guard, however, has to be concerned with the Defensive Lineman facing him on the line of scrimmage as well as a possible very large charging threat coming from the side by a Corner or Linebacker. This means a player in the Guard position risks getting hit from the side while engaged with the opponent in front of him, which increases the chance of injury significantly as the threat is from multiple directions simultaneously.

Because their roles are so similar, the safety equipment for Guards has a lot of similarities to the Center's equipment. However, you will notice that their job is different from that of a Quarterback now that we have read through the function of each position, and the safety equipment options could be expanded to be much more specifically designed for people in each position. Their jobs aren't the same, their equipment could be equally different from one another, and perhaps as a result end up offering a greater level of safety to everyone on the field.

There is rarely a cookie cutter answer to every question in life, and when it comes to football safety gear we have a system that encourages the gear for each position to be largely the same. Shoulder pads might be a little bit different, helmets and faceguards are slightly different, but perhaps these differences should be much more pronounced. A redesign with some serious thought as to the job function of the person wearing the equipment on the field seems like a logical activity. Perhaps the league should work with some mechanical engineers who specialize in these types of projects to work on the concept. The safety level of every position can be increased with specialized gear, of that we have no doubt.

Offensive Tackle

The next guy(s) on the offensive line are the known as the offensive tackles. They are the outermost linemen. Depending on the throwing hand of the quarterback (left or right) the opposite offensive tackle has one of the most important jobs on the offense. He must protect the quarterback from his blind side, this is vital to the tempo of the offense.

We have all seen plays where a defensive player comes at a quarterback from behind and violently tackles him to the ground. That is a blindside hit, and they are some of the hardest hits on the field, and typically come as a complete surprise to the guy being thrown to the ground. Quarterbacks who suffer from one too many of these during a game, or season for that matter, get nervous. So, to keep the passers state of mind at ease, and to prevent loss of some serious yardage because of a threat that the Quarterback couldn't possibly scramble his way out of because he didn't see it coming, these players are vital and must do their job flawlessly. They must be trusted by the QB, so he can focus on what he must do to move the ball down the field, and not worry about some unseen, large, fast moving threat he can't see due to his stance as he prepares to pass the ball. If this position has a player who is performing poorly, the momentum of an entire offense can be quickly disrupted as the QB will be nervous and not focused down field.

These players need to be able to move quickly, be agile, and be able to handle any size, fast moving, very determined player coming their way. As a result, their pads need to be protective from any direction, as they can take a hit from either side or the front. They will commonly be knocked to the ground, potentially in a very violent way as someone on the defense wants to get to the QB. Remember, the faster the defender, the more energy in the hit. This equates to a higher potential to be knocked backward. Being knocked backward causes an increase in the probability that your head will be whipped into the ground and the head-ground impact could be hard enough to be concussive in nature.

There are statistics that show, and some player interviews confirm that a great number of concussions are actually caused by the field.

As we indicated earlier, there is a type of gear that has never been fielded in organized gameplay. A position such as this and several other linemen may benefit from a helmet that is attached to the shoulder pads with some kind of shock absorbing structure, perhaps even some kind of hydraulic shock absorber. This could limit, or at least slow down the impact onto the ground for the head and be built in such a way as to allow the players head to still pivot enough to not miss fast moving defenders coming in from the sides, as anything that causes them to miss one of these guys, as we discussed, will disrupt the momentum of the offense and potentially cause a team to lose the game.

Running backs

There are two types of these. They are known as the tailback and the fullback.

What is the difference you ask?

A fullback is usually a larger person, whose

duties are split. Sometimes he is a ball carrier, usually this is in cases when you need to power through a short distance to either get a first down or cross a goal line. In other cases, they are blockers, for either the tailback or the quarterback when he plans to run the ball himself or do a handoff for a larger pickup on a running play by the fast running, typically smaller tailback.

A tailback is usually the guy that is the furthest behind the line of scrimmage and is almost always lined up behind the fullback. He will almost always (hopefully) average more yards per carry than the fullback, but that is simply because he has the fullback blocking for him, thereby creating an opening for him to run through. They tend to be one of the more visible players on the offensive side of the ball. This is because they have the longer runs, sometimes they are receivers, and they are typically one of the players who score a lot of touchdowns; therefore, they get a lot of camera time and make the game highlights more often as a result of their higher scoring frequency.

Their safety gear should be unique, and considering they can get hit from any direction, and they need to be fast, not to mention agile at any time makes it problematic to increase their protection level and keep them safer than they are today as more protective gear would weigh more and may impact their mobility. It is possible to create light, yet highly protective equipment. It typically costs much more, but there is only so much technology can achieve at a certain price.

To make the protection matters a bit more challenging they can and will be driven into the turf any number of times during a game.

Part of these players remaining agile will include his need for the ability to keep their head swiveling. That implies that no larger, bulkier pads can be added if he is going to do his job properly. Certainly, his helmet must be protective from every side, and only a further study of typical and far more common hits can show where padding can be enhanced to make a difference.

Certainly, anything limiting head movement would be problematic.

There would be a challenge in connecting the shoulder pads to the helmet in a way that limits the range at which his head swivels so that he can see defenders coming quickly and easily. The development of a piece of safety equipment to achieve that goal is going to be mechanically difficult, and hopefully not necessary assuming an improved helmet system can be developed for people performing this task on the field. But using currently known technology there is no helmet designed specifically for this position, and while advances are being made, there is a long way to go. The rate of concussions caused by these players hitting their head on the ground after a tackle is not inconsequential. There is more work to do, and far more questions to answer than currently available technology can achieve. We hope this starts the discussion for these players.

Wide Receiver

These guys are pass-catching sprinters. They run pass routes quickly and attempt to lose the defender who will be sprinting along with them at every turn. It is a contest between the two of speed and agility.

They typically line up nearest the sideline and go down some predetermined route based on the play call. These routes are so the Quarterback knows where to look for them amidst the fast-moving chaos of the field.

Simply put, their job is to get to a position where they have lost their defender, can catch the ball and move forward as far as possible, hopefully to the end zone, without being tackled.

They are among the faster players, so let's think about this in relation to that energy equation we previously discussed. They are moving as quickly as a human can under all that gear. They defenders covering them are also moving quickly. Two fast moving objects hitting each other hard are going to cause a lot of kinetic energy to go someplace; we are on a mission to not have it go to someone's head. Their collision with one another may not have that much kinetic energy as their momentum is all in the same direction and the energy is the total velocity involved, therefore it is the difference in speed between the two that matters, but they are going to hit the ground at some point. That energy, that field cushioning (or lack of it), will become important at this stage when it comes to a potential head injury. More on that when we discuss artificial turf.

Typical hits for wide receivers are from the side or rear. The challenge with these players is that we can't really do a snazzy equipment addition like attaching the helmet to the shoulder pads, as their heads really need to get to any kind of position quickly. Think about it, these guys need to look back over their shoulders, to the sides, and front, in every direction possible very quickly. Any kind of attachment and mechanical equipment that impedes that ability to move their head quickly will not be used to help people in this position prevent injury…ever.

Better padding in the helmets will help, perhaps a different type than has been used before, but also a superior mechanical structure designed to take a hit.

What can be done with these structures you ask? Why is the physical structure important?

There are types of mechanical structures (shapes) that can absorb or disperse energy better than others. But wait, there is more. Not only is it possible to design energy absorbing materials like pads so that it is possible to absorb hits more efficiently, but through some careful design it is also to send that energy somewhere other than directly through to the head. For instance, it can be spread out over a larger area, but it can also be sent to a particular location as well.

Think about it like a push pin. Pushing your thumb into the bulletin board doesn't do much, push your thumb on a pin and you go through it. With a similar (yet spun around and reversed) set of physics, the energy can be moved around to other parts of the helmet and sent into specific layers of the padding system to aid making sure those structures either stop or slow that energy transmission down. That is certainly a better option than transmitting it full speed into the players head. Remember that speed is the largest contributing factor when it comes to kinetic energy.

Tight End

Tight Ends are a hybrid of just about everything on the offensive squad. They can play the role of everything from a wide receiver to a lineman. They block, run, catch, and everyone occasionally, on a trick play they may even throw a forward pass. These guys should know the offense every bit as well as the Quarterback and must know the job of everyone on their side of the ball on any given play call. It is a truly dynamic position.

Because of Tight End's hybrid approach to the game, an amalgamation set of equipment is necessary to protect those players. We first need to consider a light attachment between the helmet and the shoulder pads, but Tight Ends need to stay agile, flexible, and fast. Their helmets must protect from every direction, and their equipment must prevent their head from having rapid impacts with the turf.

You have probably noticed that we have mentioned the turf so many times because it presents a problem, especially artificial turf. Artificial turf is responsible for concussive hits frequently enough that, for every ball carrier on the offense, any kind of equipment which prevents or at least limits the players head from hitting the turf with as much speed as players are witnessing today should be considered. If it doesn't exist in the currently market, perhaps some entrepreneurial person reading this book has an idea they can develop. It is worth thinking about.

Defense

This is the squad on the team that has one job and one job only...stop the other team from scoring.

That's it, nothing else really matters to these players. With that in mind, we need to understand who they are, and how they line up as compared to the offense. Then we can worry about the safety equipment needs for these guys whose job is similar to that of the Incredible Hulk (to smash) and how changes should be made so they can do their jobs and stay safe.

Defensive Line

These are the very large men that line up directly across from the offensive line. It is their mission in life to grab hold of and throw to the ground anyone carrying the ball in their proximity, hopefully causing a huge loss of field position in the process. Some of these guys desire to achieve this goal with as much violence as permitted by the rules of the game because it will rattle the nerves of the offense and will throw off not only their confidence but tempo.

The psychological game matters as much as the physical aspect. That is something that the casual observer who has never played may not realize.

Think of it like boxing. If you can get in another boxer's head before the bell rings it is easier to win once the round begins. Muhammad Ali was the best in the world at the psychological part of boxing. A wise man once said (George Foreman) that if you had to fight him, you better shut off all radio and television broadcasts for a week or more before the fight. Then get out there in the ring, and once there you still must face down a great boxer, but at least you would be on even footing with regards to the psychological game.

Football is similar in this regard. There is a psychological game that goes on that exists within the physical one. If a quarterback or running back is planted into the turf much harder than expected multiple times that "head game" isn't going to go the way the offense wants it to.

What does that have to do with concussions?

Simple, the defense doesn't necessarily want to injure someone, but they sure do want that player to remember they took a hit, and who gave it to them. Therefore, there is a balance that must be struck in the rules between what is and isn't permitted on the playing field. However, based on how the human head works concussions will be a potential part of the sport, and almost any sport until we get the equipment (including a field) designed to solve this problem.

How do we know? Soccer, a far cry from football on the contact level, has a greater number of concussions that we see in football every year. Well, sure you say, look at how they hit the ball with their head. Well, interestingly most of the concussions come from when a player falls to the ground and hits their head on the turf. We talked to a few former college and one former professional player and they all agree, the turf is a problem, hitting a header isn't. Running the kinetic energy equations, the physics supports this conclusion.

Defensive Tackle

These men are at the center of the defensive line. They push on the offensive line, try to get them to move backward, fall over, or get past them by any legal means so they can get to the Quarterback (or any other ball carrier). Once these gargantuan men get within arm's reach of the ball carrier, they will put him on the ground, and not in a friendly "let me help you lay down and take a nap" kind of way.

It may seem like a simple task but remember there is a group of huge offensive lineman trying to stop them from accomplishing this goal.

When it comes to injuries, and especially head impact related injuries these players are not usually going to receive hits to the back of the head, even from their head hitting the turf. They spend their career moving forward, or at least trying to. One specific method that may be helpful to prevent long-term head trauma is to do the same smart design thinking we did with respect to potential new equipment that might be useful for the offensive linemen. One of these (and we hesitate to think of this because someone will complain) is to double up on the padding in the front of their helmet. We do not want to limit their protection in the back, but they are obviously going to have more frequent hits to the front. It only makes sense to take those frequently hit areas and offer a little something extra. There are likely additional ideas that exist but given that they are typically hit from the front, and they repeat that hit often, it only makes sense that the protections should focus on where the hit is going to take place. Also, the head should be slowed gradually so that brain sloshing around inside there can gradually, rather than abruptly come to a halt. Just like when you brake your car slowly rather than quickly.

Defensive End

These are the men at the edges of the defensive line. They are typically large and very fast. No matter the play call or evolution of the offense, the Defensive End's job is always the same, stop the ball from moving forward, and if possible, make sure it moves backwards, but under no circumstances will it move forward. That means every play they either attack the Quarterback or the Running Backs when they run to the edge of the line.

It cannot be stated enough, these guys are quick, and to be feared as one of them is on the Quarterback's blindside and can inflict a serious case of QB nerves if things go his way. It is worth mentioning that he is going to do his level best to make sure happens, and if he is good enough at it (and assuming he is at the NFL level) his paycheck is going to get bigger. They are a vital part of the defense, and possibly one of the most important guys on that side of the ball.

Their safety equipment should also be tailored to their position. Because they are more mobile than a defensive tackle, they may get blocked by some fast-moving offensive squad player who is out to protect the quarterback. A noble effort by the offense, but one we must protect the man from.

Therefore, it is likely going to be a better solution to have their head protected all around, and prevent that ever-present problem of hitting their head on the artificial turf. It would not be out of line to consider adding some kind of attachment between the helmet and shoulder pads (see a pattern developing here?) which could use hydraulic pistons to slow down that impact.

If shock absorbers can work on cars, they can be miniaturized using modern mechanical engineering techniques and used for player safety. I know at this point the connecting the helmet to the shoulder pads is getting redundant. It isn't that we are pushing that as the solution, merely as an option. Something must be done to slow down that whiplash effect and this would work when implemented properly. If there is a better way, please build one and bring it forward to the football community.

Middle Linebacker

The Middle Linebackers are usually the play callers for the defense, and they line up directly behind the defensive line. They personally must be responsible for stopping running backs, covering short pass plays, or rushing the

Quarterback during a blitz. They really are kind of a "jack of all trades" on the defensive side of the ball. They are fast, agile, and strong.

Given the nature of their job, they may be hit from the side or front by a blocker and will often be shoved to the ground. There is a large potential for them to hit their head on the field from any direction. They may also be hit by other players (offensive blockers) and those collisions may cause additional head injuries. Their head should be protected from every direction, and probably attached to the shoulder pads if at all possible, to disperse that energy even further. Remember when we said we wanted to give the energy somewhere else to go? That hydraulic concept is one of many possibilities.

It is worth noting that yes, we realize we mention head-field impacts a lot. Ask anyone who has ever played football or soccer, head to turf impacts happen often. They are something that almost every sport must be concerned with if the concussion problem is going to truly become only a minor issue in organized sports (even youth sports). We have offered up a solution for limiting the velocity of those impacts, but artificial turf (discussed later) can also undergo an evolution to improve the softness without damaging the ability of players to run on that same surface. Cushioning is a good thing for head injuries, but have you ever tried running on a pillow? It isn't that easy. In other words, artificial turf has to be tuned to a specific set of parameters and given that there is some data to support that concussions in athletes tend take place less often on natural playing surfaces than on artificial ones we have a reasonable model from which to design an improved artificial surface. More on that later.

Cornerback

The Cornerback's job is to cover the wide receiver. They stick close in order to break up a pass, or if there is a completed pass, they are the man responsible for stopping that forward progress as quickly as possible after the reception. They may even occasionally intercept a pass and become ball carriers themselves.

In the case of an interception, they will run in the opposite direction from the initial flow of the play as quickly as they can while portions of the offense (now turned defense) run towards them at top speed. When this happens, the resulting collisions have the potential to be high speed and more physically damaging than most.

The nature of their injuries on a normal play will mirror that of wide receivers. Therefore, any safety precaution taken for those players should be mirrored on Cornerbacks, with the exception of that interception situation. In these cases, their potential for injury is higher.

That potential comes from the energy equation we explained earlier. When two players are running in the same direction that speed of collision isn't as fast. When the Cornerback intercepts the ball, he runs the opposite direction, straight at most of the offensive squad who wants to stop their progress. That speed differential is at some of the highest witnessed in the game. It will be challenging to add any kind of protective gear that a wide receiver doesn't have as it would encumber their ability to cover their assigned offensive player, but if there are ideas out there the leagues at various levels should be receptive.

Safety

A Safety is the last line of defense. If an offensive player breaks free, this is the guy that handles it as the last line of defense. If he fails at his job, and the offensive player breaks past his position, you can bet that there will be points added to the board.

Due to the nature of this level of responsibility, he must be ready and able to do just about any job on the defensive squad. His safety equipment should be as protective as possible and still allow him to move around the field like a cornerback. In the long run, the safety equipment used in this position may become some of the most technologically advanced (and likely expensive) on the field. He should likely have aspects of all the safety features for concussion prevention discussed. There will always be a risk playing this game, but whatever can be done to limit that risk should be tried.

Special Teams

Special Teams are the specific squads on the field when the ball is about to change hands as a result of kickoff or during a field goal/extra point attempt.

The kickoff (or punt) is where these players are usually going to experience an injury.

These plays are *the* most dangerous in the game. Thinking about the physics equation again involving velocity, these plays have the potential for players to highest speed collisions possible by those athletes on the field.

Why is that, you ask?

Let's focus on kickoffs, as punts have essentially the same problem just to a slightly lesser extent. The players are at their most distant from one another. The kicker kicks the ball, and it goes most of the way down the field and is caught. By the time someone gets to the ball carrier and performs a tackle both he and the ball carrier are, more than likely, moving as quickly as they can in opposite directions. More kinetic energy is about to be brought to a rapid halt than on any other play.

Many of these plays wind up with a ball carrier going out of bounds, which is really the safest option, but that isn't always the case. Look at some game film of those that don't and see how hard those hits are. It can be brutal.

There has been discussion of eliminating this play completely from the sport, and that (from a physics perspective) may be the correct answer.

It would certainly be the safest.

Can that change be one that allows the game to continue to be enjoyed?

Isn't the kickoff too exciting for the fans to be robbed of the experience?

Isn't it far too boring to just put the ball on the 25-yard line and get the QB to go to work?

As we have learned previously in this book the sport has evolved before. It can do so again and survive. If the kickoff is changed and taken away football will still be football, only with fewer injuries. The kickoff returned for a touchdown will go away, but there is always that first play from the 25-yard line (assuming they just start the play there). Some of those will be a touchdown as well.

The Kicker

The Kicker has an obvious job. He kicks the ball either on kickoffs, punts, or on field goal attempts. These players are rarely involved in a tackle in any way. Their equipment can be some of the lightest on the field as they are almost never doing anything other than kicking. There are even rules against touching these guys unless it is under some very specific circumstances.

Holder

The Holder holds the ball as it is kicked on an extra point or field goal attempt. Many teams will use either a Quarterback or backup QB to do this in case they want to run a fake kick play and either run or pass the ball for a first down (in the event of a punt).

The safety equipment, in this case, should be that of a Quarterback as there is neither need nor time for him to change gear for these more specialized plays.

Long Snapper

This position is exactly what it sounds like.

When a kicker is far behind the line of scrimmage (for instance on a punt) the person snapping the ball must hit a target much further back than on a normal snap. They line up just like a Center and their safety equipment should have the same considerations.

Kick Returner

This player will stand far back from the line of scrimmage. He has one of the most dangerous jobs in the game. He catches the ball after a kickoff (or punt) and runs as fast as he can directly at the other team that just took up the defensive side and are all running at him as quickly as they can to prevent any more forward progress than absolutely necessary. His gear must protect every part of his body, and his head must be given careful attention. He should have the best helmet available, be protected from every angle and again, to prevent that dangerous head-ground impact some form of connection to the shoulder pad to limit that whiplash motion that results in the head hitting the ground. The challenge is that he has to be fast on his feet, so this must be done with as little weight added as possible. This player is typically someone who would be like a wide receiver in their skill set. They are fast and mobile.

Chapter 4
The Transition to Television and the development of Artificial-Turf

It surprises some people to learn that the first football game to ever be on television pre-dates World War 2. I know what you are thinking, was television even a common thing back then? Well, no, it wasn't. In fact, television was a long way from being a success, and was still largely an experiment to see if it would catch on, which it obviously did.

That first game ever broadcast was on October 22, 1939, and there were only 13,000 or so people in attendance at the game in the stands. By comparison to today's "game day in the stands" numbers that is barely a high school game in some parts of the country.

The names of the teams competing that night might seem a little strange as one no longer exists, but it was between the Philadelphia Eagles and the Brooklyn Dodgers. No, not the baseball team who just showed up in the wrong place at the wrong time, that name was once upon the time used by a football team from Brooklyn.

Now, this was a single game, and the routine

broadcasting of games was still a thought for the future. Regular television coverage didn't occur until after World War 2, but it wasn't the same wall to wall, "see every game" kind of coverage you have today with the NFL packages available on satellite packages offering you every game ever played during a season. In fact, the ratings weren't all that star-spangled awesome as the teams would do everything that they could to get people in the stands. Baseball was still the national pastime and held the lead as far as popularity among all organized sports. At least, here in the United States. Soccer has always dominated in large parts of the world.

What does attendance have to do with television?

Well, a lot.

When you take time on your day off from work to watch a game, you want it to be exciting. You want it to be energetic, even if you are a television viewer. Watching a game played in front of an empty stadium is not nearly as interesting as one with a huge crowd, as the crowd impact is gone. Just ask Professional Baseball what happens when their stadium attendance is down.

How was a league to handle this situation?

Well, simple, they discovered that if a local team was on television, and the game was broadcast in that local market, attendance would slip. People could just stay at home, go to a bar, or go to a friend's house. The fans would find other, less expensive ways to view the game.

The solution to this problem was put in place in 1973 and continued until 2014 with strict enforcement. It stated that a home game cannot be broadcast in the local team's television market if any tickets are still available for purchase 72 hours prior to kickoff.

Ouch, that hurts. But, let's remember that the NFL is a for-profit entity, and the teams are not playing out of the goodness of their hearts. Football is a business. Ratings matter, and the higher the ratings, the better the television deals. The better the television deal, the more revenue brought into the league, the more revenue, well you see the pattern. The higher the salaries, and ultimately the bigger the Sunday sports spectacular that can be put forward for the fans to enjoy!

Now that we live in a world where the sport is televised, and in a day and time when blackouts are a thing of the past, we must focus on that all-important market penetration. It is important to understand how vital the television ratings are before we get to the league of today.

Once television came out of that experimental stage and into its "television in every home" stage football came along as one of the available things to watch on this new form of home entertainment. Certainly not every game could be seen in every home, there just weren't enough channels to carry it live. If it wasn't live people would just listen on the radio, as live is always better than a delay.

How could the league improve the number of eyeballs on the screen, and in the stands at the same time? Well, the blackouts were a good method of getting people to the game, so we aren't going to cover getting people in the stands. The real money injected into the league that supports those player contracts we all hear about on sports news shows comes from television rankings, not ticket sales. The numbers are orders of magnitude larger in one of those cases.

The financial gain seen by the league from those television deals are driven by advertising, which is costlier for companies to do in the cases of large audiences. It only makes sense, if you want people to know about your company, you must advertise on shows where the customers you want are looking. The more people looking at an ad, the better the results tend to be. The entire football industry is driven by popularity, and television is the most profitable part of that for the league. Therefore, for this book, we felt it instructive go over a few changes that were made to the game to increase TV ratings as any changes made to the sport must consider the impact to television.

Yes, there is a connection to concussions, bear with us a minute.

In order to do make that discussion meaningful we want to introduce you to a man named Tex Schramm. Without him, the league would not be in the position it is in today.

Mr. Schramm began his involvement with Pro-Football way back in 1947 with the Los Angeles Rams. This was at a time when the NFL was trying to decide if they were going to add an expansion team in Dallas, planned to occur in the late 1950s, he made it known that he wanted to run that new team. He got what he wanted and did indeed end up running the Dallas Cowboys in the early days of the franchise. While he was there instated some alterations to the game and more importantly to the playing field that changed the way football looked on television.

In that role, with the fundamental changes he made, we now take for granted he was a major influence in making not just the Dallas Cowboys, but the NFL successful on the televisions that now existed in most homes in the United States.

He did three very specific things that really pushed those all-important television ratings higher. This, as we already discussed, is what makes the league of today the business powerhouse that it is. We will enumerate these things, and then explain them in detail.

1) He made sure the flags were added to the top of the goal post.

2) He started the Dallas Cowboy's Cheerleaders as a professional, rather than a volunteer, squad.

3) He hired Tom Landry as head coach.

What do all these things have to do with a book on concussions?

Well, remember that we are trying to explain how the sport got where it is today, as it also helps us understand the concussion problem. These things will matter, and television ratings are the one thing that pulls the whole train forward…like it or not it isn't ticket, or jersey sales. It is television commercials. This set of changes by Mr. Schramm were some of the things that started to drive ratings on the road to ever higher numbers.

The flags at the top of the goal posts are far more important than you may think. If you are someone who watches football on television rather than being in the stands every weekend those flags are the only way you know there is any wind that may cause challenges for the players on the field. Sure, some announcer could tell you something like "the wind is right to left and it is fast, down there on the field it must be…" but it isn't the same as seeing the flags flutter in the wind.

If you see a kicker lined up to attempt a 45-yard field goal, there was no way to tell if it is calm wind or heavy 30-mph gusts without those things. In short, this simple change puts the television audience in the stadium (without sitting in the snow, ice, rain, cold and wind). It makes you feel more like you are there, with the kicker, right beside him, waiting for the snap, nervous about where to aim the kick so that the ball will hit the mark despite the overwhelming odds against you.

That feeling is what Tex wanted for fans. He made strides, and his spirit exists in the league today as they seek ways to improve the viewing experience for the audience.

Thanks, Tex Schramm for understanding that need of the home audience. Without this simple change, which was so innovative that it cost the league almost nothing, it would be a much different viewing experience. Think about how much difference this simple little change impacts the viewing experience. Someone else may have tried some technological jump that put a wind speed and direction indicator on the screen.

Now, in the 21st century that is easy, back then it would have been a huge challenge, if it was possible at all.

The man wasn't done finding ways to get the viewing audience more excited to watch games every week.

The cheerleading squad was next on the list for Mr. Schramm. This one seems obvious now, but it wasn't always that way. They made their debut during the Cowboy's inaugural season, but they were not the squad that would be there by the end of the decade. This initial season the squad was made of local high school students, which wasn't unusual for the league in the 60s, as the pro teams and televisions really didn't give the cheerleaders much attention.

We know, what was wrong with them? Isn't this one just obvious? Well, now it is, but we aren't living in the world of then, we are living in the world that was built by the people that came before us.

Sure, before the professional squad the young women would be there to get the crowd excited. They did the job, and that probably helped the television audience as the crowd was more excited to be in the stands which enhances the viewing experience, but that wasn't enough for the Dallas Cowboys. They wanted to break the old mold and create a whole new model for the rest of the league to follow.

During a game in 1967, there was an incident with a very scantily clad, really well-endowed woman in the stands that gave Tex an interesting idea. No, not that, please get your mind out of the gutter. Ok, at least make sure that your mind is gutter adjacent for a moment.

This woman had an outfit, and a dance routine she was doing, that caused people to pay attention to her. She was getting more attention in ways than the game.

If a woman could distract the crowd, what would happen if the television audience had that same experience? More importantly, what would happen if someone timed the cheerleader's appearances and activities in a way to occur purposefully during lulls in game play? Would it improve ratings?

Before the 1969 season kicked off, the cheerleading squad had a complete makeover. No longer would the cheerleaders be both men and women (yes there was a time when the Dallas Cowboy Cheerleaders had both), the men were now gone. The all-female squad was still made up from local high schools, but their uniforms had certainly changed (gotten smaller) and they now made television appearances on broadcasts other than the game. They even started to make those appearances on shows on non-game days. They developed calendars people could buy and hang up at home or in the office. They hired marketing directors specific to the cheerleaders, and all kinds of publicity which drove the popularity of the game for both the television audience and those in the stands. The cheerleaders started to become celebrities, and that helped football's popularity even more.

Between the 1969 and 1970 seasons, Schramm was not done tweaking things. The routines the squad performed were less like the traditional cheers and acrobatics performed by high school and college cheerleaders and become more dance-like. In order to really make this transition of the squads meet the quality the NFL had come to expect; the team hired a choreographer. By 1972 started they were in full swing.

There was one other important change. Schramm decided that cheerleaders must be at least 18 years old, and of course physically attractive as well as talented performers. With that, the cheerleading squad we know today (and has frequented television even in the offseason ever since) was born. This served to boost ratings further, and the television audience continued growing.

Why is this cheerleader bit important?

It shows just how important ratings are. The higher those ratings the better the league is doing their job. Anything to put one more set of eyes on the screen. It is, after all, a business.

What does this have to do with concussions?

Bear with us but assume for the moment that ratings are always the ultimate goal. The people watching football are doing so to escape their lives, and we love the chance to do that. We are not saying the league has done anything wrong, they are merely giving their customers (us) what it is we obviously want. If we didn't want it the ratings would not be as high as they are.

Now, for one last important contribution, Tom Landry. What can be said about him that hasn't been said before. Probably not much, but let's tie it to the television ratings discussion, and in some ways, the desire to increase those ratings has driven the concussion problem.

Wait? What was that? How the heck is that possible?

We want to take a momentary aside before we get back to Coach Landry.

It is likely that the highlights clips we all love have pushed the league to go in a direction for more dramatic hits to become a growing part of the game. Higher scoring games, faster, larger players are getting higher ratings and more exciting games. Faster moving offenses, larger men, hitting harder than ever before, all lead to higher ratings, and increased rates of concussion thanks to that pesky physics kinetic energy equation we mentioned. We already established that all the kinetic energy is going to go somewhere, bigger and faster adds to that equation by all possible methods (mass and velocity).

So yes, in a way, the growing concussion problem is a byproduct of the league wanting to give the fans more of what they want.

So, is the league at fault or is humans and our desire to compete as well as our fascination with all things violent from traffic accidents to action movies?

That's for people smarter than us, but we are saying there is likely a link with humans being humans. In other words, concussions are an unintended consequence of humans wanting to see certain things on the playing field.

The league just gave fans what the largest number of people watching the game wanted. Now, it is our job to figure out how to give the fans what they want, and keep the players safe, which we believe can be done.

What does this have to do with Coach Landry?

He may have started it all in his desire to build the best possible team, which he succeeded in building the dominant team of his time.

How did Tom Landry influence ratings, and the league of today?

Well, when Tex Schramm hired him to be the head coach of the new Dallas expansion team, Coach Landry was given a task of building the best team in the league. It was to be a team for the ages, and he did exactly what he was asked to do. When he took this posting, he approached his job more like an engineer designing a building than someone building a team. He had a deeper understanding of statistics, and how the stats of someone at one position would complement the stats of someone at another, more so than any coach up to that point in the history of the sport.

I know, boring math junk, but what does an understanding of all those statistics have to do with television ratings or a good football team. Well, apparently a lot, because he was the head coach for the Dallas Cowboys for 29 consecutive years, 20 of which were consecutive winning seasons. Not to fail to mention that every team in the league today uses his work as the basis for what is done today to build a team. They also use his work and process to establish training regimens for their players.

Tom was not just a statistician. He was a risk taker.

He had the good sense to get everyone involved

in the team to take a risk on drafting a quarterback coming out of the Naval Academy and waiting for him to finish his military service before he could take the field.

That player was Roger Staubach.

The risk obviously paid off. Roger was the cornerstone of an offense that struck fear into teams all over the country.

Between Tom Landry, Tex Schramm and Roger Staubach, along with the help of some of the most talented players on the field at the time, they ended up earning the team the nickname "America's Team."

This creates an interesting question. Were these men so good because they had natural athletic ability? Sure, there is some truth to that. But they also had the right leadership showing them what needed to be done to be successful and getting the players the resources they needed to improve.

This created a situation where people all over the nation wanted to watch them play. They weren't just a local team, they had fans everywhere, from coast to coast. They even had a solid fan base in cities that had their own team. They had higher television ratings than anyone, sold more jerseys, and other bits of merchandise than most teams thought possible. Thus, the nickname America's team.

How did Tom Landry put them in this position?

The 20 consecutive winning seasons didn't hurt, nor did the five Super Bowl appearances in nine years, or the 2 Super Bowl wins, and 5 NFC championships certainly helped. He did this by innovations at the position of head coach, just like Tex did for the rest of the team business. Between the two of them they built a more popular team than anyone thought possible. This had a byproduct of driving the team to higher ratings than had ever before been seen in the history of the league.

There were so many innovations it is hard to list them all. For instance, he built a defense to use formations and styles than had ever before been tried. The now common 4-3 defense was his innovation. It allowed the defense more flexibility to react to whatever the offense had up its sleeve.

Long before most NFL teams had strength and speed training programs, and coaches who specialized in these things, Coach Landry brought in Alvin Roy and Boots Garland to focus on these aspects of athletic performance. This resulted in, pound for pound, a faster team than elsewhere in the league. Remember the thing about speed and kinetic energy?

Wait...hold on, we all know football players need to be fast. How was Coach Landry different?

Well, yes, to outrun people. It makes sense. I'm not saying anyone intended things to get this way, but in the drive to win he built a faster team than anyone considered possible at the time, and the concussion problem has become an unfortunate byproduct of the league adapting to their customer's desire for speed.

Velocity matters for that kinetic energy equation. He wanted to win, the league wanted ratings, they did the logical thing and everyone else followed along.

He recruited kickers from soccer, such as Rafael Septien. That resulted in a team with a kicking game that was challenging to match. He pulled players who were known in track and field, like Bob Hayes who was once called the fastest man in the world to play wide receiver.

He was also the first to add a person (Ermal Allen) whose job was to analyze game films of other teams. That's right, before Tom no one watched game film to train or develop a strategy for a specific game.

In other words, he wanted to leave no stone unturned.

Bigger, faster, better prepared. That was Coach Landry. But he wasn't done there.

He hired trainers to teach players Tae Kwon Do

in order to better learn body movement techniques, not to mention they would receive training on new methods of taking people to the ground. That last one might be useful on the football field.

Apparently, some players got pretty good at this. Most people who played in the NFL at this point in history will say a Dallas Cowboy defensive squad member, Randy White, got very good at it. He could put a hit on you during a Sunday afternoon that according to multiple sources you still felt on Thursday.

Not, a bad set of innovations.

Ratings were up. Hits were harder, guys were faster. The modern league was in full swing, and the next generation was about to be born.

Now, let's remember that he had Roger Staubach as the Quarterback for a decade. Roger was loved by everyone, on and off the field. He was a patriot, played a clean game, and he gave everything he had every week as did everyone on his team.

He was also someone who did charity work, appeared on TV, worked with kids, and ran his own business in the off (and somewhat during) the season. He really was all American and was beloved by many fans.

Between Tex, Tom, and Roger, as we mentioned

earlier, they deserved the nickname America's Team. After all, they had a quarterback with the nickname Captain America in the pocket, it just made sense. Now, who came up with the name? That was a narrator of the team's 1978 highlight film by the name of John Facenda.

That team nickname was a blessing and a curse all wrapped into one little two-word phrase. It made every team in the league want to prepare harder to play the Cowboys than any other team. It happened for years, everyone wanted to beat them, they all came to play hard every week, yet Tom Landry still managed to win.

The ratings skyrocketed. Everyone watching loved it. The team was tough, it was fast, and thanks to Tex and his work on the non-team side of the broadcast, they were fun to watch.

The Cowboys would be "the game to see" on a weekly basis for large parts of the football viewing public. Even if you rooted for another team who wasn't playing the Cowboys that week you may still tune in hoping to see a good game.

Now, that brings us to the late 1960s. The quality of television broadcasting was getting better, and the league wanted to get the "look" to be better and better in any way possible. More cheerleaders, more close-ups, more highlights, an even greater spectacular event every week than the week before.

The league finally had its look, and the popularity was rising, they continued to refine a few things. The teams were getting faster, the hits getting harder, and the overall energy (kinetic and support) was going up.

The playing field was up next on the list of things to be improved.

Artificial turf became the answer to grass fields that didn't always look their best on television. As early as 1966 NFL stadiums started using the stuff. It has evolved and changed a bit over the years, it has even somewhat improved, but it still has some challenges.

Why do we care?

It can't be said often enough that ratings drove the desire for better-looking fields. Artificial turf was an inexpensive way to achieve that goal, while giving the viewing public what they wanted.

These artificial fields have several layers of padding under the green stuff that resembles natural grass on the top which is what we all see on television. There is typically a padding layer on top of the concrete layer that is underneath the surface. That padding may be a multi-layered, multiple material approach. Basically, several types of materials are usually in place between the green top layer and the concrete foundation. In modern fields ground-up tires are a common approach to provide the upper layer of padding the players hit after every tackle.

The challenge with this type of padding is that those little rubber balls start out under the field in an evenly coated layer all over the field. During gameplay these can get shoved to the side in higher traffic areas, and that means the players are landing on the harder layers below that nice padding designed to stop them from being injured by the ground.

The ground, the artificial turf, even with the little ground up rubber pellets, is harder than most people think. It can, after being used many times, become significantly harder in some areas than natural grass even if it starts out softer.

Think about the situation we have learned so far. Players are bigger, they are faster, and they are shoving each other to the ground harder than ever before. If that ground is hard enough, and their head whips down after the body hits the ground and the head pounds that turf, guess what, the turf can and will cause the concussion. If you are lucky enough to hit something with all the padding in all the right places, it works pretty well, sort of, if the turf and padding aren't working exactly as designed due to natural wear and tear, well, all bets are off. This head ground impact (which can still happen on natural grass, although it is different on artificial turf) has been shown to be the cause of many head injuries from high school up to the NFL level.

How can we fix that the problem?

More research and development on padding that could go under that artificial turf would be a great place to start. The padding needs to be something that could be both affordable and safe for player's health. Something that doesn't get shoved out of the way to offer protection in some parts of the field, but not others, and responds the same as natural turf when you run on it and cut a corner. That has nothing to do with brain health, but it does make a difference to knees, ACLs, and ankles which are also injured as a result of playing the game.

As can now be clearly seen, the search for higher ratings led to a series of changes in the sport that had an unfortunate set of unintended consequence.

Is the whole concussion mess the league's fault as some people are claiming?

Or was it the fact that the league was just trying to give the viewing public what they wanted, in other words, giving the customers what they want.

What business doesn't want to give the

customers what they want?

No business can be successful telling customers what they want. That is not a formula for success, and no one can argue with the success and popularity of the NFL.

One final point that seems relevant to make with specificity, as thus far was have only alluded to it, is that the size and speed of players has changed over time. Back in the late 70s, most players were physically smaller than they are today.

For instance, Tom Landry had a guideline for the largest a player should be at various positions:

- Line Backers
    - 6 feet 2 inches and 225-lbs
- Defensive Line
    - 6 feet 4 inches and 265-270-lbs
- Offensive Line
    - 6 feet 3 inches and 265-lbs
- Wide Receiver
    - 6 feet 0 inches and 180-lbs
- Tight End
    - 6 feet 3 inches and 235-lbs
- Defensive Back

- 5 feet 11 inches and 170-lbs
- Quarter Back
  - 6 feet 1 inch and 190-lbs

He did have that speed training program, but even the speeds back then were not the same as today. Today's players are faster than ever.

Here are a few examples of just how much bigger today's players are:

- Defensive Line
  - 6 feet 5 inches and 345-lbs
  - Runs a forty-yard dash in 4.9 seconds
- Linebacker
  - 6 feet 4 inches and 225-lbs
  - Runs a forty-yard dash in 4.5 seconds
- Offensive Line
  - 6 feet 4 inches and 325-lbs
  - Runs a forty-yard dash in 5.2 seconds

The players that were on the field 20 years ago were big and intimidating. The guys that play today are larger, faster, and even more intimidating. We can thank conditioning coaches and new training techniques for the speed, and possibly some of the size, but we must understand where the desire for this came from, and that is the fans which are humans.

It is part of are psyche and as we learned earlier came about thousands of years ago with the Greeks and Romans.

Will it all stop with where things are today? Well, not if history is any guide.

The highlight reel always shows the most dramatic collisions on the field, as well as the most dramatic scoring plays. The ratings are driven by this ever-increasing desire of the viewing public to see more of this type of thing. The teams have given the public what they want, nothing more, nothing less. Now, we must look at any way we can possibly fill that need for the viewing public to get what they want and still allow for these men to play safely. It is possible to be safer than we are today, and still fulfill the public desire.

Chapter 5
Keeping Players Safe

Now that we understand the game and had a short history lesson which helped us understand some of the reasons behind where we are. It is time to understand if it is at all going to be possible for this game to be played while limiting people from experiencing concussions at the rate and severity happening in the league today.

We want to start by saying there is no one answer, there is no single solution, no shortcut available that will fix the situation. We now understand that there was no one cause, and there can be no one answer. We didn't get here overnight, and we can't get out of this situation overnight.

For example, changing to a better helmet alone, some advanced design with space-age materials, is not going to solve this problem. Now it may sound like we are trying to say this is impossible, we don't believe that it is. There is always a way to solve a hard problem. Remember, as we said earlier, if human beings can send people to land on the moon and bring them back to earth using the technology available in the late 1960s, we can make playing football safer using the knowledge and technology we have available to us in the 21st century.

Hydration

According to a Harvard Medical School publication keeping your body hydrated is important to maintain the proper function of every system in your body, including your brain.

How in the world can drinking enough water (or some form of sports drink) and brain health be linked? Ever get a headache, drink a cup of water and feel better?

Remember earlier we mentioned that Cerebral Spinal Fluid inside the skull offering some cushion to the brain, and we will get to that in a second, but it goes further than that one pesky answer (as always).

Your brain is comprised of a lot of different things. Roughly three-quarters of your brain is a fluid. As a result, when the human body is dehydrated the brain will shrink a bit in volume. This is the cause of the so-called dehydration headache.

This lack of fluid in your body can alter your brain function in several ways. The impact on a football player wouldn't necessarily be from every symptom known to the medical community caused by dehydration, but some side effects are decreased alertness, fatigue, and confusion. If you are suffering from these symptoms and sitting in your living room watching a football game on television, you may find it challenging to follow along, but you aren't really in any danger. If you are on the field, among all those fast-moving large men, you will find yourself on the ground, having gotten there due to some act of violence. This is likely to happen more often than you or your coaching staff is going to like.

Let's dig a little deeper and see how these symptoms may impact performance and increase your chances for a concussion during a game.

In 2011 there was a study that found dehydration caused by exercise-induced sweat led to a stronger increase in blood oxygen level dependent response when performing an executive function task. The translation of all that to regular English is that, given the limited availability of the brain metabolic resources, these findings suggest that prolonged states of reduced water intake may adversely impact executive functions such as planning and visuo-spatial reasoning.

That last part is particularly important to a

football player. If your visuo-spatial reasoning is off or even slowed down a bit, and you are running from a 6'5" 250-lb defensive player, you will be on the ground, probably hard. That hit, which may not have occurred had the player been fully hydrated, will have consequences. That consequence may be a concussion.

Recall that cerebral spinal fluid (CSF) is the fluid that surrounds and protects the brain. It is the thing that cushions the brain as it swishes back and forth inside the skull (also a protective structure) and slows the impact with the side of the skull in the event of a hit. If that fluid level drops, the likelihood of a concussion increases. Research has shown that a 2 percent reduction in hydration (otherwise known as someone who feels thirsty) results in a potentially significant decrease in CSF levels. One report in a peer-reviewed journal claimed the CSF level can drop by as much as 10 percent, while others agree that there is a link between the two but will claim a smaller ratio. That means, one way or the other, if you are dehydrated, the brain is less protected by CSF and the brain itself is smaller in volume than normal.

In the case of a brain that is smaller, with less CSF in the system, the velocity of the hit of the brain against the side of the skull will be higher, therefore the amount energy that must be dissipated is greater. You guessed it, that means the potential for concussion, and the severity will be higher.

In other words, taken as a whole, dehydration, or improper hydration can cause an increase in the likelihood of a concussion. Not only are the body's natural defenses diminished, but the brain function is in a state that could allow for more impacts to happen because the information processing of certain types (visuo-spatial) is impaired. We don't know about you, but we would want our visuo-spatial reasoning at its peak when trying to avoid an NFL defensive player intent on throwing us to the ground.

Conditioning

Staying in peak physical shape is one way for athletes to avoid injury (including concussion).

It almost seems like something that doesn't need to be said. But let's dig into what that really means, rather than just glibly throwing out some kind of headline to grab attention.

Staying in top physical shape is like keeping your car moving. If you are an athlete (professional or amateur) and you are not in the best shape possible, then go out and ask your body to move as fast and as hard as it can one day per week, it isn't going to end well. If you aren't in peak shape you could have a blow out of some kind.

Think about a high-performance car as an example. If your engine (or a muscle group) is putting out 1,000 horsepower, but your transmission (a joint in your body) can only tolerate 100 horsepower before shattering it isn't going to end well.

In order to avoid injury, treat your entire body as a system. It all needs to behave at peak performance. Have you ever done an exercise for your neck? If you were going to spend any time playing in the NFL, you better put it on your to-do list.

That is the kind of attention to detail needed to compete in this sport at the highest level and have any chance to remain injury free.

Keeping things in tune, from the high school level through professional is a key to avoiding injury. Not only will a muscular body bounce back better than a non-muscular one after a collision, but if your entire body is in tip top shape one body system (muscle group) that is in peak shape, won't cause another one to start to fail. If you want to compete, you need to be firing on all cylinders.

Techniques

The most common point in a football game

when a concussion occurs is when a play comes to an end. If that is in a tackle, someone falling to the ground, a player being pushed out of bounds, whatever it is, these play-ending moves are typically when the most severe concussions happen. Linemen are a different story, and we will get to that in a second.

Let's go through these instances of what happens when a defensive player catches up to the ball carrier, there are several ways that interaction can happen. The ball carrier can be shoved out of bounds, in which case there is likely no injury, and this end to a play is common.

Tackles that occur in the open field are where we want to focus for this part of the discussion.

Just in case you are not completely familiar with it we want to define what we mean by the word tackle. It is the physical act of holding a player on the ground, wrestling them down, or knocking them off their feet to the ground. Basically, any method of getting an offensive player off their feet and on the turf, thus eliminating forward progress is considered a tackle while playing football. If you do some of this to someone outside the football field it would be considered a mugging, please don't do that.

Occasionally these are very hard, sometimes

they are not. It just depends on the situation.

The higher the speed of the collision, knocking someone off their feet is the problematic hit. The style of tackling has specific rules.

The rules are changing for tackling in connection to the concussion crisis. "Head's up" tackling is going to be part of the answer.

In the case of a defensive player comes in with his head down, battering ram style, is far more dangerous for everyone involved.

In this case, depending on the position relative to the ball carrier the helmet can be used as a weapon. Let's assume the defensive player can move much faster, and both the ball carrier and the tackler are in a position where they may get hurt, badly.

The defensive player is opening himself up to all kinds of potential back injuries, on top of the concussion potential. Yes, it is indeed possible for him to be the cause of his own injury. Keeping the head up while tackling limits this potential.

This body position allows the defensive player to see where he is going, therefore he is far less likely to hurt his own head. Second, his back will likely stay straighter with his head and eyes up. Ever see what happens to a curved battering ram? That kinetic energy that enters one place is going to keep moving down the ram until it finds point of less resistance where it can exit, or bunch up. The curve better not be in your spine. If it is, some discs are not going to be happy about it.

Technique matters. Listening to coaches and keeping the fundamentals of the sport as good habits throughout the time you play is extremely important. It could prevent an injury.

Artificial Turf

If you are getting hit there are good and bad ways for this to happen and paying attention to what you are going to land on also matters. It matters enough that we want to make sure the turf offers the proper landing zone to the type of hit expected.

Not all of this can be blamed on the field. A strong neck is going to help with this problem. When you are hit with intent to prevent your forward motion, it is likely to be a hard enough hit that your head is going to whip around, just like whiplash in a car accident. That back and forth rapid head motion that we have all seen a Quarterback exhibit when hit from the blind side can induce a concussion, as well as neck problems even without anything else offering a potential for injury. But wait, this gets worse.

When being tackled, especially in the case when you didn't see it coming, a ground impact is going to occur. Not only can your head bounce around and hit your shoulders, but it can, and in many cases will, hit the ground (watch a few replays and you will see what we are talking about). If it is a sufficiently hard enough impact that your head bounces around it may actually hit the ground (or bounce) several times thanks to that whiplash effect.

Would you be surprised to learn that the harder the ground the higher the probability for a concussion? Various studies have shown that somewhere in the range of 15.5% of concussions occur when a player hits their head on the field. That is a minimum, and the number could be, according to other studies, considerably higher. But let's go with the smallest, most conservative estimate. That means that more than 1 concussion in 10 is caused by the field itself. It is also known that the numbers of concussions on artificial turf fields and natural grass field are not equal. The artificial surfaces produce more of this type of injury every time.

If the problems of the artificial field can be reduced, is it possible to get to a point where that number is reduced, and only 1 in 100 concussions is caused be the field?

It just might be possible if we properly engineer

the field. Either way, whatever the numbers that can be achieved, it makes sense that we understand the issue, and we should try to reduce the number of head injuries caused by the playing surface.

Artificial turf fields when they are first installed are softer than at any other time. In other words, as they age their "cushion" will not be the same as the day it was installed. After they are played on for some period of time, they will become harder. The ground, natural turf, has an advantage in that we know where the "padding" (aka dirt) is going to be under all that nice green stuff we look at on television. It doesn't move. The same can't be said for artificial turf.

Remember when we mentioned those ground-up tires earlier in this book? When the field is prepped for a game those ground up little bits of rubber will be in one position. Every time a player runs across the field they get shoved around a little bit as a result of heavy guys running from one place to another. From time to time they will be shoved completely out of one location. That implies that there will be an uneven amount of padding under the playing surface. In some places there may be almost nothing, and these locations will be much harder. *This is especially problematic in the higher traffic areas of the playing surface, where players are more likely to be tackled.*

If it is problematic, why did artificial turf even become a thing? Well, it looks great on television, never turns brown, and is always in season. It may not be the best for players health, but it helped ratings.

Was this an intended or unintended consequence?

The league runs on ratings. There is no way to believe that the league decided to install the stuff and in some back office a group of league executives hoped it would increase the injury rates. That wouldn't make any sense. But it does look good, that can't be denied.

In short, once again we are in a position where the league gave the viewing public what they wanted, and ratings increased. The customers got a better product. Now, can that product be improved? Can we build an artificial turf field that is the same hardness as natural grass, and does not get harder over time while maintaining an awesome appearance?

Yes, we can achieve these goals. Advances in materials science indicate that this is possible, and testing of new materials is always happening. In many laboratories around the nation methods have been discovered to "tune" the properties of a host of different kinds of materials (including padding) to meet a certain set of specifications. Someone just must put those scientists and engineers to work, which does cost something, and the fields may be more expensive to install, but we can do it.

The league has examined some and will always be looking at ways to improve fields. We don't want to leave anyone with the idea that no one is making an attempt at fixing this situation. We merely want to say that perhaps a more organized method of going after this problem and trying to come at a solution from a different direction could reach the desired conclusion at a faster pace.

One thing we also believe, is that if this problem is more widely known, there may be an entrepreneurial padding expert out there with an idea. That idea may solve this problem.

This isn't a new problem. It is known and has been for some time. There have even been former players who have invested their personal money in companies that specialize in more advanced artificial turf. The turf people play on ten years from now will be better than what we have today. The fields will improve, and now that it is known that it contributes to concussions (and ACL injuries) new padding could reduce or at least limit these injuries, and we are confident someone will solve this problem so that all fans of the game will be comfortable with their sons becoming part of that gridiron tradition we have all enjoyed for so long.

The Helmet

The helmet is basically a series of different structures designed to work synergistically to protect the players head. There is an outer layer which is typically a hard plastic shell which is outside of a padding layer (or layers). It also has a facemask which is a series of metallic bars across the players face.

Helmets weren't always what they are today. In fact, during the early years of football, there were no helmets.

The first helmets were used in the late 1800s and were made from soft leather, technically moleskin. They quickly evolved into a padded leather that and was quickly replaced with a hardened leather in the early 1900s.

The leather headed players stuck around until the 1950s when the introduction of polymer materials was shown to be much safer. These original polymer helmets still had no face mask, that addition didn't happen until the mid-1950s and quickly resulted in fewer broken noses, and virtually eliminated people getting their teeth knocked out (yes that did happen).

The concept of the helmet in the early days was just to prevent skull fractures. Concussions didn't enter the thinking. Today the helmets are designed to stop skull fractures, broken bones, broken teeth, and yes, traumatic brain injuries, also known as concussion.

The original polymer helmets had a thick padding inner layer. These evolved into a helmet that had inflatable pockets which would cushion blows better than just padding layers and would reduce concussions.

Then, in the early 2000s, some helmets started to change materials to a thermoplastic urethane. This is a material that has many properties including elasticity, resistance to abrasion, and is longer lasting than some of what was being used previously. There is some data to suggest that this material cushions the head even better than others.

These safety evolutions will continue into the future. The helmet used ten years from now will not be the helmet of today. It will be safer and prevent more concussions than ever before.

The more we understand the problem, the more we can keep players safe. It does no one any good to keep these problems secret. That will result in stifling innovation, and just like Tom Landry when he built the Cowboys, safety equipment needs an innovative revolution.

Maintenance of Pads

Did you ever have a pillow that when you first got it was your favorite pillow to sleep on? It was fluffy, soft, felt good, it was just the best thing ever. A few months later it wasn't your favorite and was kicked to the curb when a new pillow came to town.

Think about a set of safety pads that are great that first day they are used. They are cushioning the blows, they do a lot to absorb the hit. Think of them like a pillow. They age, and sometimes not well. The hits a player receives on week four of the season are not going to be protected by a pad that is as protective as it was during week one of the season. Collegiate and professional athletes have the benefit of new pads for every game (or close to it), but how often are a high school football player's pad refreshed or replaced, if ever?

Pads age, and sometimes not well. Each team and manufacturer that has not already done so should offer a guideline for replacement. Perhaps even a sensor can be built into various types of pads to tell the user when it is time for some maintenance. If we can build such sensors into a refrigerator to tell me when to replace a water filter, we are certain modern-day scientists and engineers can come up with something simple for pads to do a similar task.

There are many more ways to look at padding and safety equipment. What we wanted to do was start the conversation going in a new direction. It is all too easy to blame one group or another for the concussion problems being seen today. It is harder, but far more worthwhile to work together to solve those problems for future generations to enjoy the game.

Now, to better understand the problem, we want to move on to some interviews and discussions with former players to get their perspective on how the game has evolved. We also wanted to get their opinion on what might be done in the future to improve the situation.

Chapter 6
Jim McMahon

When writing about the long-term impact of concussions we wanted to reach out to Jay's list of friends and get some expert opinions. Who better then Jim McMahon to kick things off. Jim is the co-founder of the Players Against Concussions foundation which was created with the specific goal of making the sports world safer. It is an interesting concept, and what we are trying to do with this book is inform current and future players (as well as parents) with as much information as possible. For only when we are fully informed on a topic can we train properly and prepare ourselves for what is to come on the playing field.

Jim is a former NFL Quarterback who was on two Super Bowl winning teams. The first of these was Super Bowl XX where he was a starter, and the second was Super Bowl XXXI as a backup to Brett Favre.

After playing at Brigham Young University he was in the NFL for 14 years, including:

- Chicago Bears from 1982-1988
- San Diego Chargers in 1989
- Philadelphia Eagles from 1990-1992
- Minnesota Vikings in 1993
- Arizona Cardinals in 1994
- Cleveland Browns in 1995
    - Practice Squad
- Green Bay Packers from 1995-1996

That is certainly a long list of places to play. Along the way he managed to pick up some interesting awards and achieve a few highlights that stand out in addition to those two Super Bowl rings. These include:

- The 1986 Pro Bowl
- The Brian Piccolo Award in 1982
- NFC Rookie of the Year in 1982

- NFL Comeback player of the year in 1991

To say he can speak from a position of authority when it comes to taking a hit is putting it mildly. He took many over the years and had some really interesting stuff to tell us.

Part of the point of this book is to give you a perspective of what living with what Football can do to you body from the perspective of a player long term.

Jim has been vocal on the long-term impacts of Football on the human body, and he was not quiet on certain topics. In fact, Jim is not known to be a reserved individual. So, with that, let's see what he had to say.

Tim:

"Jim, thanks for taking the time to talk with us. If you could go back in time, knowing what you know today, and could tell yourself something at the start of your rookie year about injuries that only a seasoned veteran would know, what would you say?"

Jim:

"Not to play through the damn things. Back then you had to play, the contracts were all incentive laden. I needed to play to make money, so I took pills, I took shots, whatever it took to stay out there on the field.

"Once I lacerated my kidney, and tried to play through it. What the hell was I thinking.

"Now it is a different league because base salaries are higher."

Tim:

"Interesting. Playing with a kidney injury like that is certainly something I wouldn't have done. How did conditioning change your susceptibility to injury?"

Jim:

"It certainly helps. You have to be in shape. In football you have to condition your body to take the hits. You see some injuries now because people don't get hit in practice like they used to. So, at the game their body isn't ready for it."

This was a common answer from people. Your body gets used to taking a hit. If you don't condition it to do so, when you take a solid hit you will be much more susceptible to injury. For various reasons practices are no longer at full speed in today's league, thus reducing the conditioning for taking a hit versus what happened just two decades ago.

Tim:

"What type of injury concerned you the most, in other words, was there a type of injury you hoped to avoid at all cost?"

Jim:

"Not really a specific one. I was always leery of my knees because of big guys falling around all the time. A big man lands on your leg the wrong way, the little guy is going to lose. There should be a knee brace or something to protect against that."

Tim:

"What specific things helped you get ready for a game?"

Jim:

"I took as many pain pills as I could take and stay awake. I was eating pain killers like candy, I didn't want to feel anything for three hours. I would numb my body where I didn't feel a whole lot."

Tim:

"The day after a game, how much did it hurt?"

Jim:

"Depended on the game. Some games it wasn't that bad, some games I couldn't get out of bed on Monday."

Tim:

"In the time span in between games, what in your routine helped you get your body prepared for the next game the most?"

Jim:

"Whatever I needed to do, acupuncture, whatever training, weight training, massage, whatever it took. You have to be ready at that level to do whatever it takes to play, no matter what."

Tim:

"What is the worst advice anyone ever gave you on how to stay healthy?"

Jim:

"Not really anything bad, there isn't much advice to give other than be in the best shape you can be in. Fate is fate when it comes to injury. As long as you are in good shape, and you do what you are supposed to do on game day, you accept the risk and move on."

Tim:

"Would you rather play on natural grass or artificial turf?"

Jim:

"Grass, without a doubt."

Tim:

"Did artificial turf impact your game performance, either positively or negatively?"

Jim:

"It didn't make any difference. For some guys they said it hurt, but for a Quarterback it didn't matter."

Tim:

"Did artificial turf increase your number of injuries."

Jim:

"Yes. A lot of injuries happen when you hit the ground on turf, which causes a lot of problems. When you hit the ground and it doesn't give it's bad. I broke five rubs as a result of hitting artificial turf when a guy landed on me."

This is exactly what the physics of the situation suggests. We spent a large part of a previous chapter discussing this topic, and we won't review that again other than to say it is always good to have backup to a scientific conclusion.

Tim:

"Do you suffer from any pain problems today as a result of your time in the game?"

Jim:

"Every single day. I sleep about two hours at a time, then when I roll over just during the night I wake up because of my shoulders or neck. I can't sleep on my stomach, which I used to do all the time. I have pain in my shoulders, hands, and elbows. Sometimes my knees act up on me. Then with my head problems it is no fun at all. I get headaches all the time."

Tim:

"What do you do to manage your pain problems today, and do you think anything can be done to prevent the players of today from having these same problems?"

Jim:

"I don't know if you can do anything different to help

the guys of today. That is for someone else.

"For me, cannabis works really well to help manage the pain. It is the wonder plant. It is God's gift to us. I didn't know how good it was for us until I spoke to this Harvard trained doctor. It is an anti-inflammatory, a neuro-protectorate. It needs to be used more and get off the controlled substance list. It is much better for your body than pain pills.

"That, and if they legalized it, they would reduce the opioid problems we see in this country greatly.

"They won't do it because Big Pharma runs this country, so it will stay largely controlled."

Tim:

"Wow, that is interesting. I think attitudes are changing on it, but maybe things should move faster when it comes to cannabis.

"Now, just for fun. What defensive player did you fear?"

Jim:

"I wasn't worried about anybody. I knew the guys up front were going to give it their all and protect me."

Tim:

"Do you think there is anything that can be done to

alleviate the concussion problems and maintain the game's excitement and fan base?"

Jim:

"Not really. You aren't going to totally stop concussions. You can't stop head injuries. There is nothing that holds our brain in place in our skull. Certain animals have built in cushions for their brains, we don't. There is nothing that will change that.

"You would be better off taking the helmets of today off, take that weapon away from guys. Go back to the old leather helmets, that might help. If we did that the only time you get a concussion is when you hit the ground."

Tim:

"One last thing. Just for fun. What is the one question you wished people would ask you, but they never do."

Jim:

"Couldn't even tell you, I have been interviewed so often and asked so many. Maybe what's my adult film name?"

We didn't get much time with Jim, but we thank

him for talking with us. Surprisingly for a guy that suffers from so much long-term pain he didn't seem that bitter. It is like he wouldn't change things, almost like he didn't regret it, but he might do a few things differently.

He gave us some great games over the years and was certainly one of a kind in his day. That includes both on, and off the field.

One thing was certainly clear. He had no love of artificial surfaces. They may look good on television, but according to this man who spent many years playing at every level of the organized game, natural surfaces would have prevented a number of his injuries.

Chapter 7
Greg McElroy Jr

Greg was a very interesting man to speak with on this topic area. There are many things about him personally, and his life off the field that aren't well known.

First, he had full-scholarship offers from multiple schools. He graduated from Alabama with a degree in Business Marketing in just three years. As an undergraduate he was an amazing student with a cumulative GPA greater than

3.8/4.0.

He applied for the prestigious Rhodes Scholarship in 2010 (he didn't win). That scholarship is one that has been awarded to many well-known people including former United States President Bill Clinton.

He wasn't done with his academics yet. In 2010 he received a Master of Science degree in Sports Management with a 4.0 GPA. You don't get better grades than that. In September of 2010 he was named the 20th smartest athlete in sports by *Sporting News*, something that will be more apparent when we get to his interview.

He was an amazing College Quarterback and spent time with the New York Jets playing that same position.

We had the chance to speak with him in November of 2018 about concussions in his beloved sport.

Tim:

"As it pertains to injury, if you could go back and tell that first year NCAA guy something today that only the veteran player version of you would know; what would it be?"

Greg:

"Honestly, I have been pretty fortunate from an injury standpoint, but not everyone has the same experience. I would tell everyone that they shouldn't try to be superman. When you play your ego will drive you to want to be out on the field, but if you aren't and you have to wait out with an injury everyone should know that it isn't a reflection on your character. Player's shouldn't try to play through an injury. They should heal then get back on the field."

"That playing hurt idea has always gone on with team sports, and as a player you always want to be out there with your team, but it isn't always the right thing to do."

I remember in my third year in the NFL, the first pre-season game against Detroit, I played well, and then on the last play of the game I tore the PCL in my knee. The team Docs told me I was fine, and that it wouldn't get worse and just to focus on pain management. But, come to find out that it did get worse because I tried to practice on it when I shouldn't."

"In short, if you are hurt, don't just manage the pain, fix the source of the pain."

Tim:

"Did conditioning change your susceptibility to injury?"

Greg:

"Not really. Even in college our conditioning coaches had us on a whole new level. They were amazing. Looking at the things we could do in practice, or working out, and not think twice about it. Running 26 110-m dashes in a row, in 100 degree heat without worrying about it, I mean we didn't enjoy it, but we were in the best condition possible. If anything all the work we did at Alabama, our conditioning practices had us in such incredible shape that whatever little things happened we could just deal with it."

Tim:

"In the time span between games, what in your routine helped you get your body prepared for that next game?"

Greg:

"I would always do as much as I could in the treatment room."

"After every practice I would also go into the training room. As a quarterback I spent a lot of time throwing with my right, so I would go do a bunch of repetitions with my left to balance things out."

"Other than that, I used a lot of acupuncture, massage, chiropractors, and whatever else I could. There was a lot of body maintenance in between games, but it was all aimed at feeling the best you

can. At the professional level you find that each week you have to do a little bit more to feel better, and toward the end of the season it gets pretty hard."

Tim:

"Would you rather play on artificial turf or natural surfaces?"

Greg:

"Natural grass, not even close. Over the years artificial turf has gotten better, but for whatever reason it can't simulate or replicate the response that natural grass has. Sometimes the artificial stuff catches a little quicker than grass, which isn't good for the body. In the NFL more and more teams have gone to the artificial stuff. I can't remember too many games at that level on actual grass. As a player you can really tell the difference, and I really liked natural grass."

Tim:

"Did artificial grass impact your game performance?"

Greg:

It didn't really affect me as a quarterback too much, but one thing I noted is that it was really responsive to weather. One thing that did impact me was that I could really tell the difference on natural grass when it was longer, it would slow me down."

Tim:

"Did artificial turf increase the number of injuries you saw?"

Greg:

"I wouldn't say I noticed a difference to be honest, but in the NFL I saw more injuries and there are more turf fields. But it is also the NFL and it's a really high level of football. I didn't really notice a huge correlation, but natural grass always feels better. It's a little softer and has give, which turf doesn't have. The older turfs were much worse, and the newer stuff is a little softer, but nothing takes the place of grass."

Tim:

"What, if anything, do you think can be done to alleviate the concussion problem, and maintain the game's excitement as well as fan base?"

Greg:

"The biggest thing to realize is that concussions are just part of the game. It has gotten a lot of negative coverage over the last few years. The biggest issue I

want people to be aware of is that the protective equipment is getting better by the day."

"Another thing is they are trying to change player behavior with more strict penalties. I'm not sure concussions will ever leave the game, but our awareness is getting better, and will continue to improve over time. It isn't ever going to go away, and it will always be a factor."

"Injuries are just a part of sports. That is an unfortunate reality. What we need is increased awareness, the best safety equipment possible, and the way we enforce the rules all matter to have a safer game."

Tim:

"Is there one question you wished people would ask you but never do?"

Greg:

"Not really. One thing I do find a little frustrating is that there are so many guys on the field with a fascinating story. No matter if it was their childhood that led them to football, or whatever. There are just a lot of really cool stories about the players the good things they do off the field."

"It gets really frustrating to me that athletes get pained with a really broad brush, that we are all just a bunch of meat heads, it isn't fair. There are a lot of

really smart guys out there on the field. The perception of players is a problem, and those great stories need to be told rather than just focusing on the negative. I wish people would take time to get to know the human side of players a little better."

Greg is one of the smartest people to have ever played the game. He was so adamant that grass is a better surface for the game than artificial turf it was challenging to get him off the topic.

That seems to be a theme with former players, that turf is not optimal for the game. Statistics show increases in injuries on that stuff, even with all the new developments and technologies available. As we discussed earlier in the book these artificial surfaces were not developed by people thinking they would increase injuries. They were developed by people thinking that it would give the fans a more attractive playing surface.

Perhaps it is time for the sport at various levels to start to examine that playing surface and considering transitions back to natural grass.

Chapter 8
Howard Richards

Howard Richards is another one of those guys that has a hugely interesting off the field story.

On the field he played for the University of Missouri, where he is the Assistant Athletic Director for Community Relations. As a professional he played for the Dallas Cowboys and the Seattle Seahawks.

When he was with the Cowboys, he had to line up in practice up against Randy White. That, all by itself, puts him on another level of player.

Anyone who can do that and talk about it rationally afterwards deserves respect.

He was honored in 2012 by the University of Missouri's College of Arts and Sciences as a distinguished alumnus. In 2015 he received the University of Missouri's prestigious faculty – alumni award.

He has been inducted into the Missouri Sports Hall of Fame, and also the St. Louis Sports Hall of Fame. There are not many people that have been inducted into both, and those that have received both honors form an impressive list of athletes.

After leaving the NFL and prior to joining the University of Missouri as an Athletic Director Howard served for thirteen years with the Central Intelligence Agency. During that time he served with distinction and had the honor of meeting (for reasons we don't know) Nelson Mandela, an event he spoke briefly of with pride, and a true highlight of his career.

Imagine all of the people he has met in his life. It speaks volumes of his character that meeting Nelson Mandela was what he calls out as the career moment to speak of. We should mention that as a kid he had to be bussed to a school due to desegregation. Here is a man that really overcame the odds, didn't let perceived obstacles get in his way and made a huge name for himself. The conversation we had with him concerning concussions only served to solidify our opinion of the situation.

Tim:

"As it relates to head injury, if you could go back and tell that first year version of yourself something that only the veteran player would know, what would it be?"

Howard:

"Not really much of anything specific. Knowing what I know now I would probably ask more questions with regard to how do you diagnose a concussion. Like, if you suspect someone has a concussion what do you do to check that person out."

"If you go back to when I started in 1981 no one was really thinking about it. We thought we had the best equipment, and I don't think anyone or anything could have prompted that question then, but now I would tell myself to ask."

Tim:

"What type of injury concerned you the most, in other words, which type of injury did you hope to avoid most of all?"

Howard:

"I never really thought about being injured until it happened. Like in 1984 I tore up my right knee, it was the first significant injury I ever had playing the sport. It wasn't until I suffered what was thought to be a career ending injury that I even thought about it at all. Maybe it was me being hard headed, or determined, but I didn't take no for an answer and I got back out there. It took me 11 months to come back and ended up being a starter again. If you think about getting hurt, you are more prone to be hurt."

Tim:

"What specific things do you tell your players now that you are an Athletic Director so they can stay healthy and in the game?"

Howard:

"My interaction is as an AD, so I don't get too directly involved with the students. When I do get the chance to talk to them I try to guide them on proper diet more than anything. We weren't as in tune with it back when I played. I try to tell them to limit the use of alcohol as it really limits your ability to perform on game day. As a young guy you think you are invincible and these things don't impact you, but they do."

Tim:

"In the time span between games what in your routine helped you get your body prepared for the next game more than anything."

Howard:

"There was a guy, Doctor Montgomery, we called him Doctor Needles. I used acupuncture since 1982, and later on I discovered chirporactors in 1986 when I started having back problems."

"The league wasn't really into that kind of stuff then but I took it upon myself to go see a chiropractor and in two days I was fine again. From that point on I swore by them, and at the time it was not even accepted by the medical profession to go to chiropractors. Now there are more teams that use them, and yoga, and all that eastern medicine, and even holistic medicines more than ever before. Players have far more say so in their conditioning and choice of medical professionals than they ever have before, and I think that is helping."

"It was much different just a few decades back. When I played they used to give us all these pills. I was taking anti-inflammatories once and started bleeding rectally. I couldn't figure it out. I was talking to my mother and she said you have to cycle through those things or they can make you bleed internally. Those days are over, and things are getting better."

Tim:

"Did artificial turf increase your number of injuries?"

Howard:

"Yes, absolutely. The stuff was brutal. In simple terms, the way I understand it, when you see a horse run on dirt and it flies all over the place that is the force of the horse running displacing the dirt. When you play on artificial turf there is no displacement of the turf to speak of. The natural surfaces can displace a little bit. The modern artificial surfaces are a little better, but only when they are brand new. There is a long way to go."

Tim:

"Have you had any concussion concerns about long term impacts since leaving the game?"

Howard:

"Well, one thing is I did a study with Boston University. They asked me how long I played the sport, and I gave them my daily routine going back to college. They surmised that I had at minimum 550 concussive episodes, at the micro-concussive level. As an offensive lineman you hit someone ever play, practice, or game it didn't matter. You got hit often and hard. It was limited but there was always some

helmet to helmet contact.

Howard was an inspiring person to talk with. Our conversation only served to solidify much of what we talked about earlier in the book. We thank him for his time and wish him the best of luck in his continuing role as an Athletic Director.

Chapter 9
Randy White

What book on concussions, or hell, football would be complete without a discussion that includes Randy White? He was the defensive tackle amongst defensive tackles in the league from 1975 until 1988. He spent his entire career with the Dallas Cowboys.

There are more career highlights than we can mention in one place but here are a few:

- 111 career sacks
    - some quarterbacks still have nightmares
- Super Bowl XII Champion
    - He was co-MVP

- Nine Pro Bowls
  - 1977-1985
- NFL 1980s all decade team
- Dallas Cowboys Ring of Honor
- Two time All-American
  - 1973, 1974

Remember this is a guy whose job it was to get to the Quarterback, or any other ball carrier that came out of the backfield. He did this with a vengeance that earned him the nickname "The Manster," as in half man, half monster. He studied Thai Boxing under Chai Sirisute who was the founder of the Thai Boxing Association in the United States.

When asking a few retired players who they would rather not see across from them when they were playing the most common answer received from players of this era was...Randy White. He struck fear in the heart of people who had no fear. He put quarterbacks on the ground at a time before the roughness rules were what they are today, and probably shattered the nerves of more than one.

When we interviewed Randy he is exactly what you picture a defensive player being. He is blunt, to the point, direct and doesn't mess around. He is the guy you want on your side, and never want to face off against.

At one time the all-time leading rusher in the NFL was Walter Payton, a record later broken by Emmitt Smith. Walter Payton was once asked about a head on collision he had with Randy White, Payton said it was the hardest hit of his career.

Getting input from a guy who put people on the ground as hard as Randy, for a book on contact sports injuries and concussions seemed like a no brainer.

Randy was gracious with his time.

Tim:

"Randy, thanks for taking the time. We are doing this book on concussions and Jay said it wouldn't be complete until we talked to the guy who hit harder than anyone in the league."

Randy:

"No problem, anything for Jay."

Tim:

"I did want to let you know that when you bring your name up around Jay he still shudders just a little bit."

Randy:

Laughing – "Well, it was fun to play with guys like that. He was so fast I couldn't catch him anyway. In a Jay and Randy contest Jay runs a pattern, fakes me out, catches a pass and scores 25/25 times. But nice to know I'm remembered."

Tim:

"What type of injury concerned you the most, was it concussion or something else?"

Randy:

"You know, I never thought about my brain being injured. If I thought about anything at all, I guess I wasn't really thinking about getting hurt. It was just never a thought in my mind. It was something that happened."

"I was of the opinion that the harder you went, the less prone you were to injury. My concern would have been knees, if I actually had a concern it would be what happened if someone falls on your knees. In giant piles of big guys that was a concern, but I never really thought about getting hurt. I focused on playing the game."

"If I did get hurt, I did anything I had to do to get well. I guess it isn't that you have no fear, but you are brought up playing a game and told to ignore the *pain from the moment you start playing. You are conditioned from when you are a little kid to just go back in there and do what you need to do. I had a few broken bones in my fingers and I broke a foot one time. I missed a Thursday game once when I broke my foot. The next week they put a metal plate in my shoe, and got shot up and I went back out there."*

"The kid's playing today have it different. Back when I played we were conditioned to say I wasn't hurt. Today players are told you might be hurt and you better go sit down for a bit. They are told to wear special gear to save that injury. The kids today are more aware of the injury than in my day, and that will make careers longer."

Tim:

"In the time between games what did you do to get your body prepared for the next game?"

Randy:

"Percodan. Pain killers."

"That's just the way I did it. When I was playing I just thought that's what you are supposed to do. When you are a player you hate losing, even in practice. You can't go half speed because the other guy is going full speed."

"I think today you see a lot of injuries because teams practice at half speed. Then they get a lot of time off.

Then on Sunday you go out there and they ask their bodies to do something that it isn't used to doing. When you do that your body doesn't respond the way it would if you practiced at full speed."

"Another thing is that when you practice at full speed you don't get as tired during a game. When you get tired, that's when you get your ass kicked. When you are tired, you get hurt more. That's why you see more injuries late in the game, because people are tired."

Tim:

"Would you rather play on artificial turf or natural surfaces?"

Randy:

"I really like artificial turf. More of my strength was my quickness, and when you play on turf you never get bad footing. If I had it to do over I would probably say grass, but I would have to be well taken care of grass fields. The fields we played on were like concrete. You deal with the pain, but when you went down you would scape yourself up on the turf that we had, and that scrape would stay with you the whole year."

Tim:

"Do you suffer from any pain problems today as a result of your time in the game?"

Randy:

Laughing – "Of course. I have a headache right now that I have had for about a month, but you live with it."

Tim:

"What do you think can be done to alleviate the concussion problems seen around the game, and maintain the excitement and fan base."

Randy:

"I don't really know. You would have to study the data and see if the rule changes they have made are actually making the number of injuries go down. I do think that if they keep changing the rules people will stop watching because at some level fans like to watch the violence in the game. If they take that out of the game, it won't be as much fun."

"Personally, I don't like to see all these flags thrown because someone accidentally bumps into a quarterback."

"Bob Lilly once said something that I'm going to steal. Someone once asked him if he could play in today's game. I don't know if I could play in today's game, but I know these guys today couldn't play in my game."

Tim:

"One last one, just for fun. Was there any player you feared?"

Randy:

"No, I was never afraid of anyone. If I was I would never let them know, and I would probably have just hit them harder."

It was instructive to listen to Randy talk, even for just a few minutes. He obviously loves the game, and is a bit of a purist thinking we should keep it as it was formed. It is also possible that he liked turf better because when you tackle someone it hurts them more. He does get that the speed is what matters, which agrees completely with the math we discussed earlier.

One thing is certain. They haven't made too many people like Randy. He was made for football, and we are glad that he played.

As a quick follow up, Jay does believe that there was one-person Randy was afraid of…Head Coach Tom Landry.

It is very important to understand that Jay said that when he wasn't in the presence of the Manster. We haven't asked Randy if that was true, but perhaps there is something to it, neither of us want to be the one to ask a guy known as Manster if he really was afraid of someone.

It is important to note that once we spoke to Randy, we went and talked to a large number of other people. Randy has a unique way of putting things, and a very different way of looking at the game. Even the way he thinks about the game is so different we came back to him with some follow ups based on other conversations. These follow ups were even more enlightening than the first go chat, especially as is comes to thoughts on artificial turf, and how he thought about the head injury side of the sport when he was playing along with some sage words for people playing today.

Tim:

"Randy, thanks for carving out a little more time for us. We talked to a number of other former players and to a person they all prefer natural grass over turf. They say it was better for the body, helped them avoid injury and overall was better for long term health. You are the one dissenting voice. What was the difference? Was it because you got to land on all those other guys during a tackle, or was the some other reason you preferred turf to grass?"

Randy:

"When you asked that question, you have to understand I never thought about injury or pain at all. I just dealt with the pain and never even considered injury to myself a possibility. My only concern when I played was quickness, and sure footing everywhere I went. Turf gave you that, and grass didn't."

"There was this one championship game, the field was natural grass and it was really wet. It slowed me down, it messed up my hamstrings and I couldn't run. Maybe it is a little arrogant of me to say, but I really think if we had been on turf I could have influenced the outcome of that game and made it a win for Dallas. The only thing I ever cared about in my playing days was victory. Turf gave me an edge, and I wanted that edge.

Tim:

"After speaking to the Cowboys former, and NFL's first, conditioning coach, Doctor Bob Ward, we realized that he talked about martial arts being the key. He said you were one of the hardest working on that, and other, concepts he put forward. Is there anything you want to add about how being involved in those classes helped your career?"

Randy:

"Well, it was there, and it impacted just about everyone that had an open mind. It improved your

footwork, hand work. It helped both sides of the body.

"It was the kind of training that would help you make a big play, and big plays make the difference between win and lose, so any little thing you can do to get those big plays coming your way makes a difference. One play a game can be the difference between a win and a loss.

"Those classes did more than train you how to be fast, or break someone's grasp, it even keep control of a guy, they taught you how to take a hit. The ability of your body to take a hit makes a difference, and it can be trained. Martial Arts teaches that, and how to take a fall. It can really help the injury situation if people let it. Doctor Bob was way ahead of his time on this, and a lot of other stuff."

Jay:

"Yeah, that stuff was great, it helped me get people's hands off me for a few extra yards, and that Tae Kwon Do was key for being slippery."

Tim:

"Speaking of Doctor Bob, he said he pulled you aside very specifically and showed you that you had a huge speed difference between your left and right hand with your right being superior. He then said you became a man on a mission to change that. What kind of things did you and he put into a plan to make a

difference?"

Randy:

"Man, so much. He found creative ways to do this stuff. I ate left handed, he made us learn to juggle, whatever it took to improve speed and dexterity. I even would use the bathroom left handed. Try that sometime if you are a right-handed guy, it isn't as easy as it sounds."

Randy was amazingly open about his time on and off the field during his career. I think it is important for players, and those making changes to the game, to take into account the experiences of those that came up through the ranks previously.

One important thing that sticks out about him. Other than victory, nothing else mattered. He would do whatever he could to make sure his team won, and the other guys lost. It is a rare individual that will put his body and soul into something the way Randy does. He likes to win, and no one who has seen game footage can say he didn't do whatever he could to make sure that happened for the Dallas Cowboys of his era.

Chapter 10
Coach Bob Ward

Bob Ward, now 85 years old, former US Marine, Vietnam Veteran, and former Conditioning Coach for the Dallas Cowboys game us some of his time to discuss a few things as it relates to injuries in contact sports. He spent an entire book explaining his role in building America's Team in his book *Building The Perfect Star: Changing the Trajectory of Sports and the People in Them.*

Before we get to that interview, we felt it would be beneficial to give a short overview of his career in case you are too young to remember when he was involved in the NFL.

He was the NFL's first full time strength and conditioning coach. Considering that he serviced an entire team and there are now players that have their own, dedicated full time coach it was a much different league then. He took that job in 1976 (Jay Saldi's rookie year) and was offered that position by none other than head coach Tom Landy. Coach Landry wanted to focus on building a team unlike any other. He felt that proper conditioning was imperative to building one of the best professional athletic organization the world had ever seen.

He stayed in that job through early 1990, which meant he shaped an entire generation of players at a time when the Cowboys were one of the most dominant teams in the league.

Remember, at the time of our conversation Bob was 85 years old. He was as sharp as he ever was and remembers much of what he did like it was yesterday.

One thing that stuck out in our conversation is that he tied much of his NFL experience training players to the way the Marine Corp prepares men for combat. Let that sink in a bit.

Unlike many of the interviews we chose to bold face some important points that he would repeat. We did not put the repetition in the book, merely bold faced it for emphasis.

Tim:

"Thanks for taking the time to talk with us. Your career has set the standard for teams in the modern league when it comes to conditioning of their players. Let's start at the beginning. Was there something you would typically tell a rookie that worked as much as anything to get them prepared to play at the NFL level?"

Coach Ward:

"I would sit with them and tell them the truth. There is a chain of acceptability at all levels. The biggest thing in combat is that it is performance that counts. The differentiation between NCAA and the NFL is that performance is all that counts."

*"Those people that want to learn to play on the field in the NFL, and those that continue to grow as players need to know their job, and they have to be dedicated to improving. Just like in the military the more you play or practice the better your condition to play the sport, and **the more often you play the sport and condition your body for what happens on the field the less susceptible your body is to injury.**"*

Tim:

"Was there a part of the body that you considered the most important to have conditioned to the highest level possible?"

Coach Ward:

"It is an all of the above situation. Probably the one thing that is missed most is to train the body tissue. That is fundamental. They have lost sight of that reality in the NFL today. The reality of the situation is you train for what is, and that isn't lifting weights, that isn't the off field stuff, and that isn't a half speed practice. It is the on field, full speed stuff."

"Take Bruce Lee for instance, he trained for the what ifs, and in the NFL you have to do that. I always thought martial arts was one of the best ways to train for that. A guy named Danny Inosanto trained me, and he worked with Bruce Lee. I wanted to add that dimension of training to the NFL curriculum, and I went to Dan and he and I brought that kind of training to the Cowboys. We didn't demand people learn it, we just offered it as an option."

"One guy who did a lot was Randy White. We had Randy punching the beg, and we found he didn't know how to hit with his left. We had to teach him how to do that."

"Think of training for the NFL like a Venn Diagram for players, we wanted that inner most part of the diagram to be huge, so everything would be balanced."

"When you play in the NFL you need what you need when you need it, and you never know exactly what that's going to be. *You need to be ready for anything. Just like the military, when you go into battle you don't know what will happen, you have to train for every eventuality not just what might happen when you are lined up in your particular position and everything goes exactly as planned."*

Tim:

"In your opinion is there one position in the NFL that

requires the highest degree of balanced, overall conditioning, for instance are linemen different than wide receivers?"

Coach Ward:

"I would say you are looking at it wrong. If you are thinking of a linebacker, he needs to have a little of one thing, and a little of another. Offensive and Defensive Linemen don't have to be as fast, but there are times when you need a safety or a running back to be really quick, and if they don't have it, you are out of luck."

"When I was at the Cowboys I made it a generalized program that balanced everyone as far as they could be on every aspect of conditioning. We even made human movement studies a part of it. A to Z, you need to be ready to go for anything all the time when you play at the NFL level."

"Think about it like combat. In a combat unit it is the same. It isn't just one component, it is all encompassing."

Tim:

"What did you tell players to do that would help them get their body ready for the next week when they were experiencing the pain that typically comes the day after a game?"

Coach Ward:

"This was a constant problem. I came to the Cowboys and I picked up on what they were doing and just added to that. The guys that played the most had the most recovery to take care of. The day after a game is not a time to do nothing."

"I told guys to start with slow movement. A slow long jog would work to get the stiffness out. Then build that up day after day."

"Aerobics worked for some guys. We did it all to get people moving again. Some guys couldn't even run a mile and a half the day after, some of them had to walk."

"We even went so far as to have scientists come in and help me figure out what they should do because there were times it was tough to get those guys ready to go the following week."

Tim:

"Who was the athlete that sticks out your mind as the best conditioned individual you ever saw, who stood out the most?"

Coach Ward:

"Bruce Lee. Bruce Lee and Danny, who trained me, were training and even movie partners. I personally trained at Dan's place out in California. Before he died Bruce used to come in there to see Dan, I never *got a chance to meet him. He died before I got that opportunity, but from what I saw on film, and there was no CGI back then, he was the best conditioned person ever."*

"Years after he died, I talked to his Doctor, he contacted me in Dallas about something else, and even the doctor agreed he was the best conditioned person he ever saw."

"Now when it comes to football, on our team we had a lot of really hard working guys. People like Jay, Randy White, all were in excellent shape. Everyone adhered to pretty much anything I asked them to do. Randy White was probably one of the best conditioned people I ever worked with. I brought in this Thai Boxer and he would put Randy through 15 rounds of kicking and hitting to get him ready for the game. Yeah, I think if I had to say from the football side, Randy was the top of that list."

Jay:

"When Bob told Randy that he left hand was not as good as his right he became a man on a mission to improve."

Tim:

"Do you have an opinion on artificial turf versus natural grass?"

Coach Ward:

"There have been studies done and there are statistics, but if you what my opinion if you look at the potential surfaces, all the way from sand to cement you will find the right surface to play on. If you look at what surface gives the best shock absorption, what kind of absorption do you really get from turf? The harder the turf and the inability of the turf to give or slide will transfer into injuries."

Tim:

"We have spoken to a number of players, and all prefer natural surfaces with the exception of Randy White. He said turf made him quicker."

Coach Ward:

"Well, that's probably true. But if you look at like the California wildfires that always seem to happen. Once the fire subsides everything turns in to mud because of the rain that puts out the fire. With mud you slide and it gets hard to perform, but with turf you never slide."

"Natural surfaces do absorb some energy and you will run slower. With turf you will run faster. Players do want to be fast. That speed makes games exciting. The body is going to adjust the quick movement, and players are conditioning themselves only to run on turn. If we went back to grass they

would adjust, no big deal."

"Grass is better for the body in the long run. Turf has all kinds of problems, but it does stop you from slipping and makes you faster."

Tim:

"What do you think can be done to alleviate the concussion problems in the NFL and maintain the game's excitement and fan base?"

Coach Ward:

"Yes, I think there is, and that's where the emphasis should be. It is a basic skill all players need, and the reason I brought martial arts in as I don't think there is any better way to train the entire body. **The real deal with martial arts is it teaches you how to handle energy being put into your body by some external force effectively.** *It teaches you to dissipate energy and to save your body when you are hit. But beyond that it conditions you in general."*

"It teaches you to handle all the limbs properly and take the energy from a hit in ways that nothing else does. It taught the players I worked with to deal with energy no matter where it was coming from into your body. It didn't matter if it was coming into your head, or somewhere else."

Tim:

"What one thing in the NFl today would you change if you could?"

Coach Ward:

"Martial Arts is the key. Martial Arts can help with concussions, there is no excuse for not learning martial arts if you are playing at the NFL level. I came to the NFL in 1976 and if someone out there would draw on the things I put in place back then, their players would be susceptible to injury."

"UCLA is using martial arts, and look at their injury statistics and how they are doing overall."

"Of all the nuggets that I could say if I could select anything for people to learn it would be martial arts, and really learning all elements of the human body including the mind. Condition everything you can, feeling, sensing, touch, everything. Even if it is a holistic approach."

Coach Ward was gracious with his time and even sent us some additional information to include.

When it comes to acceleration it is considered by Coach Ward to be a two-edged sword. It can product fantastic things on the field, and it can also generate the physical forces that cause injuries to players. For a long time, people have considered that quickness in sports, especially contact sports gives great performance, but also protection. It gives players the ability to stop, to start, to change direction at will.

The Coach finds it noteworthy that many Martial Arts styles have devised specific techniques to manage energy. They teach artists to effectively absorb, dissipate, transmit, add to, direct the energy in a harmless direction, or even to guide the energy is a positive tactical direction.

The most important protective element any athlete can learn is not the strengthening of tissues, but the way their collective strengths are used by the Nervous System. Many elite athletes trained specific body resources, such as the ability to bench press 500lbs, but they don't think about the bigger picture. Rather than wasting time and energy in this manner, it would be more productive (according to Coach Ward) to spend time conditioning and integrating the control of all resources. The results from such a training program would reduce the negative impacts experienced by the improper handling of energy on the field and would, as a result, reduce the number of injuries will increasing player performance. That is a win-win.

According to Coach Ward's research the ability of a player to survive on the field depends on the players' playing awareness and their responses, which are their techniques for absorbing and safely transmitting energy, as the play unfolds. The second requirement is the soundness of their tissue structure and how well they function collectively. It isn't really all that surprising when you think about it properly.

Chapter 11
Roger Staubach

We wanted the final Chapter of this book to be a good one. We had a chance to talk with Roger Staubach and see if his opinions agreed with ours.

While he has his own thoughts, we think that there are a lot of ways we agree.

What can we say about Roger that hasn't been said? He is originally from the Cincinnati Ohio area, you don't get more middle, main-stream America than that. He's a Naval Academy

Graduate, a Navy Veteran, the first of only four people to win both the Heisman and Super Bowl MVP. He is a humanitarian, a successful business leader and real estate developer, we could go on forever.

He was an obvious star playing Football at the Naval Academy, or he wouldn't have won the Heisman. He could have gotten deferments from his military service, but he chose to serve instead. Not only did he do his time in the Navy prior to entering the NFL, but he served in Vietnam. He didn't just serve in the war, he asked to serve in the war. He was an officer at the Chu Lai base which provided relief for the Na Nang Air Base. While there he commanded 41 enlisted men.

We could go on and on and on about the man. But there are a few stories that sum him up in very short order.

First, he keeps up with some of his friends from High School to this day.

The first time Tim got the chance to meet him (thanks Jay for the introduction) the subject of a high school game came up. It was a game Roger was the QB for up against the High School team from Tim's fathers High School. Roger remembered the game and complimented the team.

After retiring from the NFL Jay and he have

remained friends. Whenever Jay needed anything, whatever it was, Roger has always been there (and vice versa).

In another conversation the subject of growing up in the Cincinnati area came up. It turns out one of his favorite junk food/fast food places came up as one of the go-to places to eat when visiting. We won't mention which one, but it is really an American food kind of place, and something anyone on the planet can afford to eat at. He really is that guy, he is exactly the same person he was prior to all the money, success, and Super Bowl rings.

There are a lot of them, but here is a list of awards, both during and after his football career:

- 2 time Super Bowl Champion (VI, XII)
- Super Bowl MVP (VI)
- 6 time Pro Bowl
- Heisman Trophy 1963
- Maxwell Award 1963
- Chic Harley Award 1963
- UPI Player of the Year 1963
- Unanimous All-American 1963
- All Pro 1971
- Bert Bell Award 1971

- NFL passing touchdowns leader 1973
- NFL Man of the Year 1978
- Presidential medal of Freedom 2018

There are others we could list, but this book isn't about Roger it is about the current and hopefully future state of Football. His opinion is important, relevant and reasonable. With that, let's get to that opinion.

We will approach this a little differently than the others.

Jay has known Roger since the 1970s. The two of them got together and had a conversation about concussions, the modern league versus the league of the 70s and we want to bring the highlights.

We want to say there can, and should be a biography written about Roger, not just his time on the field but his time off the field as well. He has done so much since retiring that isn't known to the public, especially for military veterans, that it really should become more widely known.

The nation owes Roger a thank you for all he has done, and it can't be said often enough, he is Captain America.

Jay asked him if he had ever suffered a concussion while playing.

He had. Roger was knocked out 6 times in the NFL, he suffered at least 3 concussions in College, 2 in high school, and took a total of at least 10 "dingers," which caused him to be administered some smelling salts and got back in the game.

The final concussion of his career was in a game up against the Rams. The play was simple, Jay (a Cowboy's Tight End at the time) was to run a pattern for a touchdown and catch a pass from Roger. Jay did exactly as he was supposed to do, caught the pass, scored 6 points and Roger was knocked out cold. Jay still has that football.

After that game he went to see a specialist at Cornell Medical School. After an exam he was told it would be best if he retired and leave the game for good.

Roger, being one of the smartest people either of us have ever met took that advice and did exactly the right thing. He left football and focused on building his business. He used those leadership skills from the field and applied them to his life off the field.

Jay and he discussed the position the league is in today with regard to concussions and how they are handling it.

Roger felt that now, as compared to back then, the right questions are being asked. The right actions are being taken. The concussion protocols, and general attitude is such that things have improved from the days when you were given some smelling salts and told to get back in the game. The fact that players, even with a minor concussion, are getting a week off to heal, is a much-improved way to handle the injury.

The subject of turf was discussed by these two old friends.

Is it better to play on turf versus natural grass?

They both agree it was natural grass.

According to them they could be faster on turf, but the impact on speed was the same to everyone on the field. Therefore, if the field was dry grass was the way to go. The falling was better, the pain of hitting the ground was reduced. The impact on knees, elbows, arms, the entire body was lessened with natural surfaces.

Those natural grass fields are harder to maintain and keep them looking good, but they are better for player health.

We wanted Roger to be our final discussion. His opinion seemed to be exactly the same as ours.

The league is asking the right questions.

The rule changes are well intentioned and going to have a positive change.

The safety equipment is better than it was.

Natural grass is the way to go for a game with as much history as American Football.

We all want the game to survive, we all want the game to improve. We hope that the changes being made are good ones, both for players and for fans.

One thing Roger, the authors and all of those we interviewed agree on, the NFL is highly entertaining, and here to stay. Nothing is going to cause it to disappear.

www.ingramcontent.com/pod-product-compliance
Lightning Source LLC
Chambersburg PA
CBHW031347040426
42444CB00005B/216